The Public Innovator's Playbook

Nurturing bold ideas in government

William D. Eggers
Shalabh Kumar Singh
Deloitte Research

Foreword by Stephen Goldsmith
Harvard Kennedy School of Government

Deloitte.

HARVARD Kennedy School
ASH INSTITUTE
for Democratic Governance and Innovation

The Public Innovator's Playbook: Nurturing bold ideas in government

William D. Eggers
Shalabh Kumar Singh

Foreword by Stephen Goldsmith

ISBN 0-9790611-1-3
ISBN13 9780-9790611-1-0

Second printing June 2009

About Deloitte Research

Deloitte Research, a part of Deloitte Services LP, identifies, analyzes, and explains the major issues driving today's business dynamics and shaping tomorrow's global marketplace. From provocative points of view about strategy and organizational change to straight talk about economics, regulation and technology, Deloitte Research delivers innovative, practical insights companies can use to improve their bottom-line performance. Operating through a network of dedicated research professionals, senior consulting practitioners of the various member firms of Deloitte Touche Tohmatsu, academics and technology specialists, Deloitte Research exhibits deep industry knowledge, functional understanding, and commitment to thought leadership. In boardrooms and business journals, Deloitte Research is known for bringing new perspective to real-world concerns.

Disclaimer

This publication contains general information only and Deloitte Services LP is not, by means of this publication, rendering accounting, business, financial, investment, legal, tax, or other professional advice or services. This publication is not a substitute for such professional advice or services, nor should it be used as a basis for any decision or action that may affect your business. Before making any decision or taking any action that may affect your business, you should consult a qualified professional advisor. Deloitte Services LP its affiliates and related entities shall not be responsible for any loss sustained by any person who relies on this publication.

About Deloitte

Deloitte refers to one or more of Deloitte Touche Tohmatsu, a Swiss Verein, and its network of member firms, each of which is a legally separate and independent entity. Please see www.deloitte.com/about for a detailed description of the legal structure of Deloitte Touche Tohmatsu and its member firms. Please see www.deloitte.com/us/about for a detailed description of the legal structure of Deloitte LLP and its subsidiaries.

Deloitte.

Member of
Deloitte Touche Tohmatsu

Printed by Printcrafters, Winnipeg, MB, Canada

"*Creativity* is thinking up new things.
Innovation is doing new things."

Theodore Levitt

Contents

Foreword

As this foreword is being written, governments around the globe face unprecedented challenges. The global economic meltdown made an already challenging set of circumstances exponentially worse for government. Public officials now
face job, housing and revenue losses on top of the still daunting list of previous
problems, including rising health care costs, global warming, crumbling infrastructure, terrorism, and immigration issues.

The greatest economic turmoil since the Great Depression will create the
perfect storm of falling revenues and increasing spending for social welfare. At
the same time, democratic governments are taking on a greater role in financial
markets and other ailing industries.

The temptation will be for government to hunker down, to depend on established approaches. This would be a big mistake.

Now more than ever, government needs to embrace innovative approaches
to daunting problems. The reason is simple: existing practices will not suffice.
To have any hope of success, governments must embrace innovation as a core
discipline, becoming adept at adopting new practices. Innovation must become
part of the public sector DNA.

In this book, authors William D. Eggers and Shalabh Singh lay out a blueprint
for how to do this. The concrete insights they offer will prove invaluable to those
public officials seeking to apply innovative solutions to unprecedented problems.
As the authors point out, innovation can and does occur in the public sector. Too
often, however, the public sector fails to actively promote innovation—a short-
coming this book can help rectify.

This book is co-published under the auspices of Deloitte's Public Leadership
Institute and the Ash Institute for Democratic Governance and Innovation at
Harvard's Kennedy School of Government. The Ash Institute was established in
1985 amidst widespread concern about citizen apathy and loss of trust in the
government. On the occasion of the twentieth anniversary of the program, the
Ash Institute sought to revisit the impact of government innovations worldwide
and lessons learned. This book forms a part of that series.

The Ash Institute has been encouraging innovation since its inception. For
example, the Institute's Innovations in American Government Awards Program
has received more than 25,000 applications from federal, state, local, tribal, and
territorial government programs and has given recognition to more than 400
agencies—proving that creativity is indeed flourishing in the public sector. Few
government agencies, however, have earned a reputation for being serial in-

novators; only a handful of them, for example, have been repeat winners of the Innovations Awards Program.

The goal of this book is to improve this track record—to help governments become serial innovators. The book describes how public organizations can develop and sustain a culture of innovation. It could not be more timely.

A recurring theme of the book is that governments have to become better at leveraging the creativity of those closest to the problem, be they employees or citizens. How can public leaders break the suffocating grip of bureaucracy and stimulate the innovation process? This book shows how through breakthrough examples such as the Development Marketplace at the World Bank and the Idea Factory at the U.S. Transportation Security Administration.

The innovation process, the authors emphasize, cannot remain a top-down, bureaucratic process, far removed from the concerns of citizens. Governments need to draw upon all their sources of innovation — employees, citizens, private organizations, and other governments — to produce regular and successful innovations.

In September 2007, the Innovations Awards Program conferred awards to its twentieth class of winners. Many of these ground breaking innovations came not from agency heads or a public sector environment that encouraged innovation. In many cases a committed group of employees championed these important innovations by setting out to make a difference and overcoming all obstacles.

Government can make a difference in the lives of citizens only by regaining their trust. This book is an important companion for those government officials looking to help make government better at nurturing bold ideas and delivering great results.

Stephen Goldsmith
Daniel Paul Professor of Government
Director of the Innovations in American Government Program
Harvard Kennedy School

Introduction

This is a book about how the public sector can develop and sustain a culture of innovation. Innovation is a discipline, just like strategy, planning, or budgeting. Like these disciplines, sustained innovation requires a methodical view of the innovation process, a view that links the mission to organizational structure, processes, and reward systems.

Government can and does innovate. Welfare reform and the dramatic reduction in crime in the United States since the mid-1990s are just two dramatic results of public sector innovation. The problem is that not enough public sector organizations accord the innovation process the sort of thoughtful, sustained attention it merits. Typically, innovation in government happens in one of two ways. Either innovation intrudes itself on a public sector organization in response to a crisis, or some individual (or small group of individuals) champions a specific innovation. In either instance, the benefits of the innovation are limited. Once the crisis has passed or certain individuals responsible for the innovation have moved on, the organization is left with no lasting capacity for ongoing innovation.

This book describes, using real-world examples, how a public sector organization can go from a culture of "innovation by accident" to one in which a sustained organizational commitment to innovation is baked into the organization's DNA.

This is not an easy journey. As things stand today, few public entities exhibit a widespread organizational commitment to innovation. The United Kingdom's National Audit Office (NAO) has conducted one of the most comprehensive studies on government's approach to innovation. It found that public agencies tend to approach innovation as a "one-off" change, using the "big bang" approach instead of a series of new approaches that make up a broader process. The NAO report found that innovation is generally viewed as the responsibility of special innovation units, rather than being a core value of the organization. Many public agencies equated certain methods of generating ideas, such as formalized brainstorming, as being central to innovation. Few public agencies viewed innovation as a systematic approach designed to take new ideas and turn them into successful results.

The dearth of government organizations known for having a "culture of innovation" stands in stark contrast to the private sector where, as Tom Kelly writes in *The Ten Faces of Innovation*, "Plenty of companies in divergent industries have distinguished themselves as serial innovators."[1] Kelly cites Google, Gillette, and W. L. Gore and Associates as three examples of such serial innovators. Government can and does innovate, but there is indeed an "innovation gap" that needs to be addressed.

In the words of Jessica McDonald, Deputy Minister to the Premier and Cabinet Secretary for British Columbia, "Innovation experts have told us that no public service has yet succeeded in establishing a genuine culture of innovation across the organization. That is precisely what we are trying to achieve in the BC Public Service. Our goal is to be an organization where being innovative is not just something we do but something we are."[2]

Innovation is a process, one that reflects an organization's orientation. An organization focused internally will be mired in the past. To create a culture with a sustained capacity to innovate requires an external orientation, a willingness to draw on all sources of innovative ideas — employees, citizens, and other public or private organizations. It requires an understanding of the innovation process, and a commitment to strengthen any weak link in the cycle of innovation, from idea to implementation to diffusion.

In an era of rapid shifts in technology, consumer demands, and public sector challenges, a capacity for organizational innovation isn't a luxury — it is an imperative. The ability to innovate is the ability to adapt to an altered environment, to learn, to evolve.

This handbook is organized around three crucial aspects of the discipline of innovation:

- The Innovation Process
- The Five Strategies of Innovation
- The Innovation Organization

The innovation process

Innovation can be thought of as having a cycle with four phases: idea generation and discovery, idea selection, idea implementation, and idea diffusion (figure 1). It is in the last

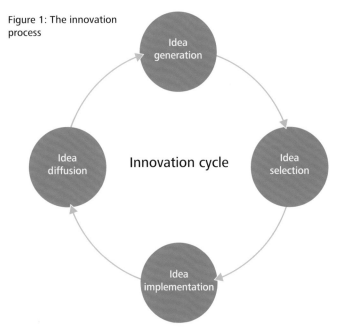

Figure 1: The innovation process

Idea generation

Idea selection

Idea implementation

Idea diffusion

Innovation cycle

Innovation strategies

1. Cultivate
2. Replicate
3. Partner
4. Network
5. Open source

Organization structure
Support strategies to innovate

three phases that innovation often gets derailed in the public sector. Innovation is at times considered synonymous with a new idea; however, until the idea delivers desirable results, it cannot be considered a successful innovation.

Chapter 1 describes the innovation process in detail and explores the four stages of the innovation cycle:

Idea generation and discovery — Numerous organizations, policy entrepreneurs, and opinion leaders regularly propose changes in government based on their understanding of the public sector environment. One result is that governments have no dearth of ideas on what they should or should not do. However, idea generation has to be more systematic if it is to deliver valuable results. Many government agencies have either ignored employees as a source of valuable ideas or have not done a very good job bringing in ideas and innovations from outside. Excellence in generating ideas requires defining shared goals that, if met, would make a difference to the organization as a whole, looking at

what other jurisdictions are doing right, and connecting with customers to understand their expectations and unmet needs.

Idea selection — After you generate ideas, you need to select the best ones. How do you decide which ideas are worth pursuing? This question is crucial for government agencies, which often have a hard time defending new ideas in the face of multiple stakeholders with the power to shoot them down. Opening up the evaluation process and using new approaches to tap into the "wisdom of the crowds" are critical to effective idea selection.

Implementation — Once selected, an idea still needs to be refined and executed. If good ideas are not converted into new programs, processes, or practices, people will stop generating them. Some of the key factors to successfully implementing innovations include:

- Giving employees and outside partners a stake in the results
- Creating customer feedback loops
- Ensuring effective communication between leadership and the line organization
- Incorporating implementation of

good ideas into strategic thinking at the managerial level
- Clearly defining a mission against which progress can be assessed.

Diffusion — The last stage in the innovation cycle is to diffuse the innovation throughout the organization and to affected stakeholders. The United Kingdom's Technology Strategy Board, which identifies key technology areas strategically important to the country, uses several mechanisms to diffuse innovations. For example, it has created close to two dozen "knowledge transfer networks" around noteworthy innovations. These networks bring together people from academia, business, finance, and technology. They work to generate innovations, facilitate knowledge exchange, and inform the government about issues that advance or stall innovation, such as regulations.

The five strategies for innovation

Serial innovation also requires strategies for tapping into the creative wisdom of employees, citizens, and external and internal partners (figure 2). While innovations in government have come from all these sources, most governments, and, to be fair, many private sector enterprises, do not have a consistent approach to draw upon all of them to produce ideas that can be executed to satisfy citizen needs, improve performance, and reduce costs.

We've identified five strategies that can encourage various sources of innovation, and help governments maximize their abil-

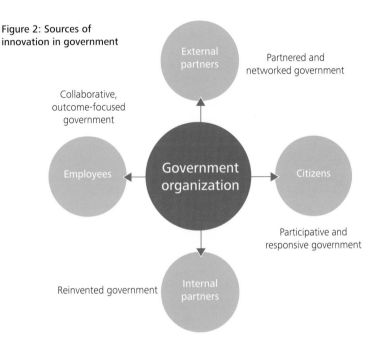

Figure 2: Sources of innovation in government

External partners

Partnered and networked government

Collaborative, outcome-focused government

Government organization

Employees

Citizens

Participative and responsive government

Reinvented government

Internal partners

ity to generate innovative approaches. These range from strategies focused on generating innovation inside the organization to externally oriented strategies that seek out and leverage promising ideas from elsewhere (figure 3). Here is a brief introduction to the five strategies:

1. Cultivate: Changing large government organizations is often about engaging employees at all levels with diverse sets of skills to generate ideas and see them through to final execution. How can public sector agencies alter their internal environment to enhance idea generation? What tools are available to motivate employees to deliver their best? The U.S. Transportation Security Administration's (TSA) Idea Factory is one experiment in idea cultivation. In April 2007, the TSA launched Idea Factory, a secure intranet site that allows employees to submit ideas for improving agency operations and processes. By the end of January 2009, employees had submitted 7,837 ideas and 69,712 comments. Of those ideas, about 39 have been implemented by the TSA. The TSA Idea Factory is an example of one tool that governments can use out of several options to cultivate innovation discussed in Chapter 2.

2. Replicate: Truly novel innovations are rare. Rather than reinventing the wheel, it can often be more effective to replicate and adapt an existing innovation to a new context. "We borrowed and adapted several ideas from other states and cities during my tenure as governor," explains former Pennsylvania Governor Tom Ridge. "It worked well because we could see what worked elsewhere and why, and then tailor and deploy those best practices in a way that fit our state's unique needs and circumstances." Chapter 3 explores the replicate strategy and suggests ways to adapt appropriate innovations from elsewhere.

3. Partner: In today's world, no organization can specialize in all areas nor should they aspire to do so. The need for both new resources and new thinking drives growing interest in partnering among government agencies, and among government, private industry, universities, and nonprofits. Partnerships let governments test new ideas quickly. They also help agencies overcome bureaucratic and financial constraints, allowing them to attack long-standing problems with novel methods and cutting edge technologies. When New York City Mayor Michael Bloomberg wanted to transform the city's underperforming public school system, he used partnerships to launch innovative pilot programs and sidestep organizational log jams. Bloomberg used funds from private organizations to test ideas before spending public money on a citywide rollout, a strategy that proved to be vital to its success. Chapter 4 covers the partner strategy.

4. Network: As opposed to partnerships,

which typically involve bilateral relationships, networks typically involve myriad organizations. The idea behind the network strategy is to utilize the innovation assets of a diverse base of organizations and individuals to discover, develop, and implement ideas in and out of organizational boundaries; better capture customer response to services; and create learning organizations. The Central Intelligence Agency (CIA), for example, funds a nonprofit organization, In-Q-Tel, to find and deliver technological solutions to the agency for a wide variety of needs, including data mining, strong encryption, and the ability to comb the Web for valuable information. More and more governments have been establishing informal global networks to tackle complex public sector challenges such as global warming.[3] The network strategy is addressed in Chapter 5.

5. Open source: In the private sector, there is a shift away from knowledge "monopolies" to open source innovation models that encourage many people to collaborate voluntarily to create solutions available for free. Two main factors have prompted this shift from knowledge monopolies to more inclusive models of innovation: rapid globalization and falling transaction costs, which make it both necessary and easier to use collaborative models. How can public sector agencies take advantage of open source models to engage large groups of people from diverse disciplines in building flexible, customized solutions? As part of an initiative to meet tough new education attainment targets, the government of

Figure 3: The strategy continuum

Internal orientation ← → External orientation

Cultivate   Replicate   Partner   Network   Open source

Ontario has employed an open source strategy with its E-Learning Ontario initiative. It built an online repository of resources developed by teachers that can be customized to local needs and made this cache of information available to teachers and students at no cost. The open source strategy, still in its infancy in the public sector, is discussed in Chapter 6.

Governments have long employed the first three of these strategies — cultivation of ideas in-house, replication of successful innovations from elsewhere, and partnerships for innovation with other organizations. These strategies, however, have often fallen short of expectations. High failure rates, slow diffusion, and crisis-driven change plague public sector innovation.

As for the network and open source strategies, the public sector is just beginning to tap these promising new approaches. The external influence for innovations surveyed by the NAO report, for example, were limited to cross-agency work and contractors as a source of innovations. Though there is growing adoption of Web 2.0 technology in government — which uses interactive Web-based applications such

as blogs and wikis to co-create content with the users — many government entities are still unaware of the power of these technologies.

Organizing for innovation

Chapter 7, the concluding chapter, looks at how to structure an organization so as to cultivate the discipline of innovation. Many public sector organizations make sporadic efforts to encourage innovation, but few implement the formal changes needed to spark transformational change. Without altering traditional roles, processes, and organizational structures, innovation initiatives become mired in bureaucracy and fail to deliver fundamental change. Creating a culture of sustained innovation requires creating an organizational structure conducive to generating innovations. Four aspects of organizational structure are particularly relevant from an innovation perspective; leaders of public sector agencies should ask themselves:

- Where are our organizational boundaries? Are contractors, suppliers, and nonprofits a part of our extended organization or considered outsiders?

12

- Do we have mechanisms to let ideas flow in and out of the organization?
- Do we have the capabilities to adopt a particular strategy for innovation?
- Is the organizational culture in tune with the innovation mechanism?
- Is the organizational structure hierarchical and opaque, or does it offer meaning, flexibility, and novelty to young entrants?

Some changes in organizational structures and cultures are necessary to make optimal use of innovation strategies. Emerging organizational models, such as the networked approach, require a bigger and more fundamental change. In this model, public sector organizations may no longer own the services they provide. Instead, they aggregate and manage services provided by others, gather ideas from anywhere, and tap talent markets far and wide. Agencies then use internal skills to adapt these ideas to their specific needs.

The future of public sector innovation

The central idea of this book is to show how to make innovation more than an isolated project or special program in the public sector. For innovation to take root, government agencies will need to take an integrated view of the innovation process, from idea generation, to selection, to implementation and diffusion. In addition, public agencies have to take a new look at strategies for fostering a culture of innovation and building an organizational structure that supports innovation. This entails developing an organizational culture where anyone can contribute ideas to help generate breakthrough innovations. It means creating organizational structures and systems that are better and faster at leveraging the creativity of those closest to the problem, whether they are employees, partners, or citizens.

Governments cannot be complacent about their ability to innovate. As the external environment changes at an increasingly rapid pace, an organization's ability to innovate becomes more crucial. As the challenges facing government become more important, closing the innovation gap becomes imperative.

Using multiple innovation approaches helps overcome weaknesses in the public sector's innovation cycle, while the organizational structure provides the bedrock for the innovation process to work. We begin this discussion in Chapter 1 with the innovation process.

"Innovation— any new idea—by definition will not be accepted at first. It takes repeated attempts, endless demonstrations, monotonous rehearsals before innovation can be accepted and internalized by an organization. This requires courageous patience."

Warren Bennis

Part 1:
The innovation process

"We started from the premise that it is
possible to run an innovation program
in much the same way we run a factory.
There are inputs; these go through
a series of transformative processes,
creating outputs."

Procter and Gamble CEO, A.G. Lafley

1 The innovation cycle

Contrary to the stereotype, many governments are adept at generating ideas. Public-private committees, citizen panels, and internal employee groups all have been used to crank out proposals for improving public sector operations. Where governments often flounder is putting these proposals into practice. In recent years, several governments have launched high-profile performance reviews, where committees of public and private sector executives reviewed government practices and suggested reforms. Some of these initiatives delivered substantive benefits, others faded from view soon after the final report was released. What was the difference? Successful innovators had a plan for turning good proposals into concrete action.

Many governments focus most of their time and resources on idea generation rather than implementation and diffusion. It is analogous to the weekend golfer who spends hours at the driving range whacking drive after drive. Once out on the course, the long practice hours invariably pay off as our hero's long, straight drives impress his golfing buddies. Once the scores are tallied, however, he finds himself dead last. Why? He lacks a short game. He forgets that the object of the game is to get the ball in the hole and doesn't focus on the little stuff. As the pros put it, "You drive for show, putt for dough."

In short, innovation is not just about generating good ideas. A good idea is only the first step; organizations then need to implement the idea and produce results. To do that, they need a clear roadmap for converting ideas into effective solutions that earn the support of stakeholders. This process view of innovation, the *innovation cycle*, typically consists of four stages: idea generation, idea selection, idea implementation, and idea diffusion (figure 1.1).

Successful innovators focus on all stages of the innovation cycle. In a recent *Harvard Business Review* article, professors Morten T. Hansen and Julian Birkinshaw argue, "When managers target only the strongest links in the innovation value chain — heeding popular advice for bolstering a core capability in, say, idea generation or diffusion — they often further debilitate the weakest parts of the value chain, compromising their innovation capabilities further."[4] The process outlined in the rest of the chapter can help build strong linkages throughout the innovation cycle.

Figure 1.1: The innovation process

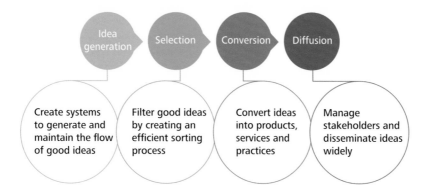

Generation

There tends to be no shortage of advice in the public sector, with academics, consultants, policy entrepreneurs, advocacy groups, and opinion leaders proposing innumerable solutions to perceived problems. Often the proposed ideas conflict with one another based on ideologies, vested interests, and political leanings.

Rather than letting occasional good ideas from the outside drive the innovation process, governments should take control of the process by developing a system designed to consistently address the unique challenges public agencies face. Figure 1.2 refers to ways in which the four sources of innovation — employees, internal partners, external partners, and citizens — can be engaged to systematically generate and capture new ideas. How many public sector employees get the

opportunity to walk up to their agency heads with good ideas? Do organizations that supply goods and services to government work as partners to deliver integrated public services? Is there a systematic way of in-sourcing ideas into the public sector? Collaboration tools like wikis and blogs make it easier to cross-pollinate ideas among employees, partners, and citizens. For instance, employees who were formerly separated by operational and organizational silos can now exchange information in Web-based open forums. Further, government agencies can import best practices from private partners to improve the effectiveness of citizen innovation panels and discovery studios.

Systematic idea generation requires clearly defining a problem — the first step in the innovation process — and then seeking the best possible solution. Gaining deep understanding of customer needs, converting those needs into clearly defined problems, and evaluating

Figure 1.2: Tools and techniques for generating and sourcing innovative ideas

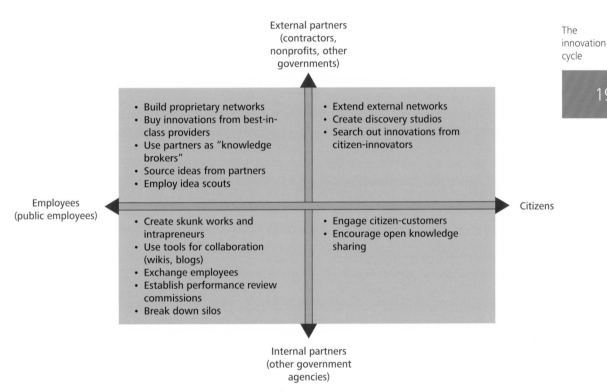

how developments in one area might affect other areas: these steps in idea generation help ensure that the organization can filter ideas to pursue the ones that best fit customers' needs.

The idea generation process should also challenge long-held assumptions, with an eye toward finding fundamentally new ways of doing things. Killing a few sacred cows every now and then is a great way to generate

some BHAGs (Big Hairy Audacious Goals).

For a team or organization that seeks to become good at idea generation, defining a shared goal is important. It helps focus attention on what needs to be achieved. The cultivate strategy plays a primary role here with special focus on engaging employees in discussion forums. Technology can be an enabler of this process through wikis and blogs. Shared goals help focus thinking on the kinds of ideas that would be embraced and make a difference to the organization as a whole. They also create commitment to the team effort by identifying how individual work relates to the shared objectives. Defining these shared objectives helps build understanding across the organization, as does identifying customers and their needs.

There can also be an outside-in perspective on idea generation: the organization can look at what other jurisdictions are doing right, what their partners are telling them, and connect with customers to understand their expectations and unmet needs. One example is the recent "innovation exchange" program between the city of London and New York City. London offers its expertise in dealing with issues like congestion pricing and climate change. New York City will share its experience in improving access to services through 311 and other technology initiatives. In the words of New York City Mayor Michael R. Bloomberg, "New York and London have a special relationship as two of the world's greatest cities: we not only compete with one another, we learn from each other. No matter where in the world you're mayor, the goals are always the same: clean streets; strong schools; thriving businesses; and, most important, safe neighborhoods."[5] As a part of the program, the cities will exchange employees to spread ideas and strategies. Exchange programs for employees provide an excellent way of ensuring they are not trapped in stovepipes that block the generation of new ideas. It is also useful in refining ideas by determining the applicability

and feasibility of an idea in a new context.

Outside-industry benchmarking can further help to unearth business innovations that can be applied to a public sector context. When Vodafone launched an initiative called Project Wow! to improve its retail stores, call centers, and customer service in general, it looked outside the telecommunications industry for innovative solutions. This benchmarking project helped Vodafone identify best practices they could adapt to better serve their customers, from Dell Computer's B2B technology service site to Ritz Carlton's world-class approach to customer service. The best practices were then mapped to Vodafone's particular needs. The result was a set of innovations not seen before in the mobile phone industry, such as a mobile squad for VIP customers and radically redesigned stores.[6]

Solving some problems requires input from multiple disciplines. Defining the problem, then engaging citizens and businesses to suggest solutions can be an effective approach. One example is the research cluster formed by Australia's Commonwealth Scientific and Industrial Research Organisation (CSIRO) to take a multidisciplinary approach (demographic, lifestyle, and neuroscience studies) for solving the problem of Alzheimer's disease.

One final point: avoid rejecting ideas too quickly. Ideas need time to develop; premature rejection of ideas will hamper the idea generation process. An idea has to be nurtured to explore its full potential before it is subjected to rigorous risk assessment and other forms of evaluation. Brainstorming sessions need to be facilitated so that group dynamics — aggressive individuals or a coterie shooting down good ideas before they have been sufficiently explored — do not come in the way of the idea generation process. Employees and managers should not feel pressured to censor or water down their ideas. The rigorous assessment process should be relegated to the next stage, when ideas are selected for further development and implementation.

Selection

How does an organization decide which ideas are worth pursuing? How do you select ideas that are big, bold, and transformative, while also being feasible and workable? These questions are particularly important to public sector agencies, which often have a hard time defending new ideas against multiple stakeholders who might say "no." Budget constraints also limit the number or nature of ideas governments can pursue. Selecting a few ideas out of multiple options, therefore, requires an efficient, transparent, and integrated approach where a wide range of people are actively involved in the selection process, and the solutions selected are aligned back to the business needs of the organization. This is why the In-House R&D Network at the Bureau of Motor Equipment of New York City Department of Sanitation allows worksite committees of mechanics to adopt proposals and implement changes within the scope of their operations.

In hierarchical systems, ideas can die fast. When only a single person or committee at the top of an agency decides which ideas move forward, many ideas may never get anywhere. To give good ideas a fair chance, a more open and less hierarchical process is needed.

The World Bank's Development Marketplace is one such successful process. The idea is simple: people with good ideas are looking to attract funds, and people with funds are looking for good ideas. Compared with a centralized decision-making process, this market offers a much more efficient way to move good ideas into the pipeline.[7] To develop new strategies to alleviate poverty, the Bank brought together 121 employee teams with ideas to sell with prospective buyers — senior executives from the World Bank and private organizations, and respected leaders from the nonprofit sector. In a single day, 11 ideas received funding from a total budget of $3 million.

One of the ideas, which received an initial $265,000 grant, resulted in the Global Alliance for Vaccines and Immunization, which promotes vaccination for the most damaging diseases in tropical countries. The task that the alliance set itself is to help reduce by two-thirds the number of children in poor countries who die before they reach age five. According to World Health Organization estimates, the alliance prevented 2.9 million deaths between 2000 and 2007 and protected 36.8 million children with basic vaccines.[8] One of the lessons from the Development Marketplace has been that organizations do not need to spend billions of dollars to make worthwhile contributions; smaller amounts may go a long way toward making

Figure 1.3: Tools and techniques for idea selection

22

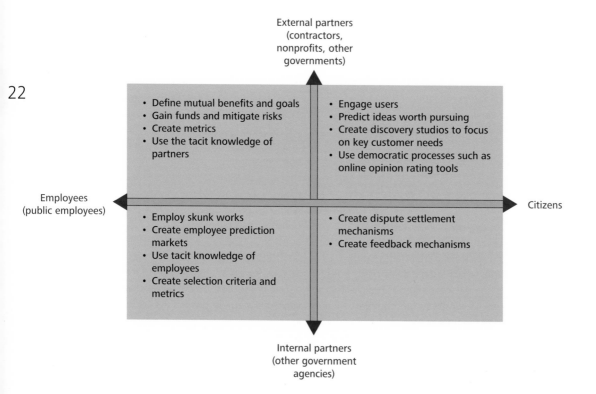

External partners
(contractors,
nonprofits, other
governments)

Employees
(public employees)

- Define mutual benefits and goals
- Gain funds and mitigate risks
- Create metrics
- Use the tacit knowledge of
  partners

- Engage users
- Predict ideas worth pursuing
- Create discovery studios to focus
  on key customer needs
- Use democratic processes such as
  online opinion rating tools

- Employ skunk works
- Create employee prediction
  markets
- Use tacit knowledge of
  employees
- Create selection criteria and
  metrics

- Create dispute settlement
  mechanisms
- Create feedback mechanisms

Citizens

Internal partners
(other government
agencies)

an impact on seemingly intractable problems.

Another novel approach to selecting which projects move forward was developed by Washington DC Chief Technology Officer (CTO) Vivek Kundra. In 2008 he launched OCTO (Office of the CTO) Labs, which takes a portfolio management approach to fund worthwhile projects and kill projects unlikely to deliver. Each of the city's IT projects is treated as a stock that employees can buy and sell. Projects are evaluated on the basis of management team, customer satisfaction, and how likely they are to finish on time and within budget. Similar to well-performing stocks in a portfolio management company, promising projects get more investment. Projects unlikely to meet their goals are shut down. Kundra hopes that with this approach, the aggregated wisdom of employees working in the trenches will increase the likelihood of funding ideas that actually work.

With OCTO, Kundra also aims to change the risk-averse culture in government. "I think controlled risk is very healthy," says Kundra. "That's why I created OCTO Labs. The idea was that we would throw hundreds of ideas on the wall and even if five of them survive, they will be transformative."[9]

Another serious concern in selecting ideas is that public agencies often have to compromise among multiple objectives in deciding what solutions to pursue. Several questions need to be answered in this regard: Given risks, how do we ensure sufficient payoff on our investment? How do we capture the impact of every dollar spent? How do we know which alternative to select? Too often these questions are considered too difficult to answer in the public sector context. One way to address this issue is to create metrics to help select the best prospects from a portfolio of ideas. The Ministry of Health and Long-Term Care in the province of Ontario, Canada, has done this to assess trade-offs between competing investments. The ministry has used the experience of private firms to develop a portfolio management approach designed to link innovative investment proposals to public health priorities, performance measures, and risk factors. The tools the province is developing will help it decide, for example, "Is investing in prevention better than investing in productivity improvement initiatives, such as electronic patient records?"

Other strategies for improving the idea selection process are shown in figure 1.3.

Implementation

Once selected, an idea still needs to be funded, developed, and executed. If ideas are not converted into services, practices, and programs, they may stop flowing in. If they are not properly executed, they can attract widespread criticism and perhaps even lead to public embarrassment. Strategies for making sure innovations are well executed are outlined in figure 1.4.

One issue governments often face in implementation is to incentivize a change in the behavior of their employees and partners toward an outcome-focused approach to implementation rather than mere compliance with statutes. Gainsharing (rewarding employees for improving performance and reducing costs) and share-in-savings (having partners share project costs, risks, and rewards) are two innovative mechanisms that have worked well previously to incentivize the proper execution of ideas. The share-in-savings model is typically used when the end results can be easily measured, with the benefit of lowered upfront spending by the public agency. It provides incentives to the partners to ensure that the promised benefits materialize at a cost less than the quoted price.

Governments often perform services where outcomes are difficult to measure and clear results are hard to define. Further, unexpected changes and developments can impact projects in any number of ways. Dynamic organizations remain flexible in the face of uncertainty, making course corrections in implementing innovations when needed.

Figure 1.4: Tools and techniques for idea implementation

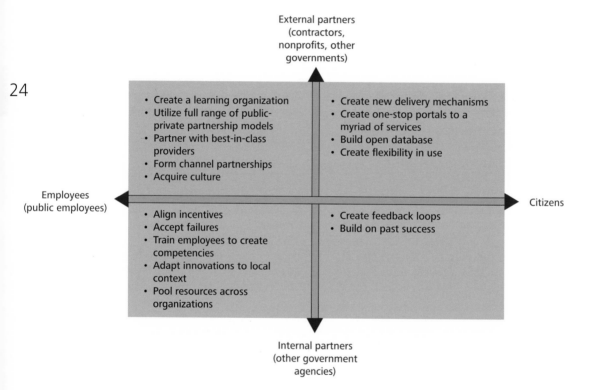

External partners
(contractors,
nonprofits, other
governments)

24

- Create a learning organization
- Utilize full range of public-private partnership models
- Partner with best-in-class providers
- Form channel partnerships
- Acquire culture

- Create new delivery mechanisms
- Create one-stop portals to a myriad of services
- Build open database
- Create flexibility in use

Employees
(public employees)

Citizens

- Align incentives
- Accept failures
- Train employees to create competencies
- Adapt innovations to local context
- Pool resources across organizations

- Create feedback loops
- Build on past success

Internal partners
(other government
agencies)

A good example of the importance of a flexible approach is the Florida School Year 2000 Initiative, a school-reform program that provided teachers a handheld device to record information on students that could be retrieved later for assessment and reporting. The program design offered flexibility and efficiency. For example, teachers can spend up to a week getting the records together to prepare student progress reports. The new technology reduced this time substantially.[10] However, the initiative ran into problems early on: the idea was dependent on emerging Wi-Fi technology that had just become affordable but had unique limitations in the context of Florida schools.

Because Florida schools often double up as hurricane shelters, their walls are made of high-strength concrete, which were impenetrable by

Table 1.1: The public sector change paradox

How the public sector often thinks and acts	How change actually works
Detail-oriented planning with locked-in execution	Focus on outcomes — what is the real objective?
Requirements gathering focused on what exists	Define and commit to the principles of the new design
Strict adherence to defined requirements	Flexibility to adapt to changed circumstances
Inability to change course	Incentives for leading and supporting change
Postmortems of project failures	Detect and correct errors as they occur
Diffusion of accountability and responsibility	Clear accountability and responsibility supported with commensurate resources and decision making powers

the wireless technology. Instead of locking the contractors and the technology company into a dispute, the project team decided to move to a wired network. They shifted to handheld devices that had high information storage capacity and could dock with the network at the end of the day to transfer information. By making this mid-course correction to overcome technological limitations, the project remained on budget and was considered successful.

Failure to take into account new information is not the only problem governments face in implementing innovative ideas. Multiple sign-offs and complex administrative structures obscure accountability, create delays, and make it difficult to recognize and reward those leading the innovation effort. This may, in turn, result in the loss of experienced employees to other organizations where they may feel better appreciated for their efforts.

Getting better at implementing innovative ideas means understanding better how the change effort works (see Table 1.1).[11]

Efforts to measure progress need to take into account the completely different way a change program works from everyday operations. Some suggested measures of innovation performance include:

- Listening to the community to get their feedback on new ideas
- Analyzing the number and depth of pilot projects for new service or process development
- Monitoring and reporting the number of projects meeting objectives.

These measures of performance ultimately have to flow from the mission of the organization, and unless the mission changes to accommodate these measures, innovations in the public sector environment will flounder. If the mission is complicated, riddled with conflicting goals, and difficult to make operational, innovative performance will be compromised.

Defining the organizational mission is often a leadership issue; it requires a fresh look at the role of the public sector agency and strong political will to change it. For instance, dissolution of a public service or institution of full-scale privatization is not a simple management issue that can be dealt with by middle managers. As the Thatcher government in the United Kingdom demonstrated in the 1980s, it generally takes a very clear mandate from the public and a strong leader to overcome vested interests. The Thatcher government was able to overcome stakeholder interests to privatize many state-owned enterprises and functions such as steel, telecommunications, gas, electricity, and even water. But effective leadership is also likely to be needed for less sweeping ideas, including those generated at frontline staff or middle-manager level. This means that the role of leadership is not merely to "think" or "strategize" but also to implement.

Leaders help transmit an idea generated by an individual or a small group to the entire organization. They also build a coalition for change. Many frontline employees already know what needs to change, even if they are not sure of the steps in the process of change. For example, Steve Kelman, who led the initiative to reform the U.S. federal government's procurement system, estimates that around 18 percent of the employees were active advocates of the reform even before its launch. Pressure from the top did not create these change advocates; it merely helped them to come out into the open. These employees in turn influenced a second group to support the initiative and their ranks swelled to around 40 percent soon after the initiative was launched.[12] This brings us to the last stage in the innovation lifecycle: diffusion.

Diffusion

Diffusion is often considered the same as replication. There are, however, important differences between the two. Replication, the topic of chapter 3, is a strategy used by public agencies to identify and adopt innovations spawned elsewhere. Diffusion refers to spreading an innovation throughout an organization or organizations, often with a push from above or with the help of external agents. Successful diffusion requires solving at least three challenges: gaining support from all stakeholders (especially top leadership and citizens); breaking down organizational silos; and overcoming organizational reluctance to change.

Gaining buy-in for an innovation in the public sector is much harder than it is in the private sector because governments are responsible to multiple stakeholders. It's not just a matter of getting citizens to accept an innovation. A government agency also needs to win over employees, unions, and political parties. Figure 1.5 provides several approaches governments can use to diffuse innovation.

Gaining support from the political leadership and other employees can be a critical factor in diffusing the idea through the organization.

Figure 1.5: Tools and techniques for diffusing innovation

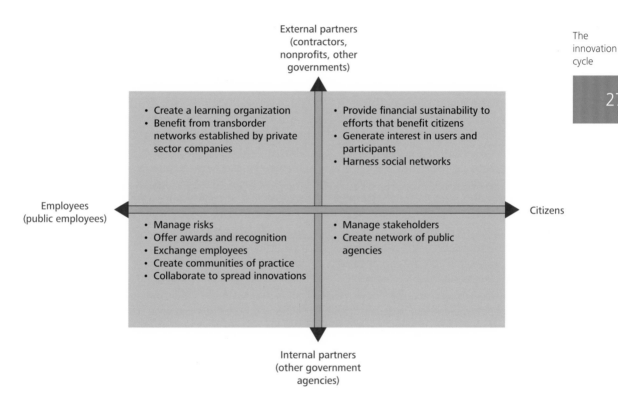

One way to encourage diffusion is to "create a buzz" around successful innovations. The Florida Department of Children and Families, which provides various child and community care services, including licensing facilities, slashed customer wait times by 45 minutes, shrunk turnover, and saved $11 million annually. After their efforts earned them several awards, word spread fast, and soon other state and federal agencies were copying their efforts. This is what Ken Miller, the founder of the Change and Innovation Agency, a firm that helps organizations radically improve performance, has termed "guerilla warfare" for innovation.[13]

Programs with proven track records tend to meet less resistance than untried ideas. Therefore, publicizing a program's success in one unit can help to diffuse it to other parts of the organization. Once the word is out, the innovation will be adopted more easily by the entire organization and possibly by other organizations. You can position programs as successful by sharing the news of employee appreciation or by highlighting outside awards. Third-party validation can have a powerful impact on the acceptance of new ideas. For example, many programs that win the Kennedy School's Innovation in American Government award, awarded annually to 10 projects that set a standard for excellence, are replicated nationally and internationally.

Organizational silos can be another barrier to diffusing innovation in public agencies. Government employees tend to work within strict organizational boundaries and make independent decisions about which ideas get adopted. Encouraging employees to work in other organizations that have implemented innovative ideas can help them learn how to deploy those ideas in their own organization. Private sector organizations that deliver solutions in a variety of contexts also can serve as agents to diffuse innovations. They can help ideas traverse organizational hurdles, and even transfer innovative practices from one country to another.

Finally, diffusion of innovation often must overcome apathy among citizens and political leaders. Publicizing evidence of success is critical to building faith among citizens and political leaders that public money is not being wasted. The emergence of Web-based social networks also may help agencies ease the introduction of innovative processes, particularly when they require changes in customer behavior. Public agencies have struggled with marketing these changes in the past. Many e-governance initiatives lacked uptake as citizens continued to conduct government transactions in person or via telephone. This meant that some of the savings expected from online service delivery did not materialize. In the future, using social networks to build support and understanding of new initiatives may lead to faster acceptance.

"What is now proved,
was once only imagined."

William Blake

Chapter in a box

Innovation is not just about generating good ideas — that's only the first step. Organizations also must select the best ideas, implement them, produce results, and then diffuse them.

Idea generation: Clearly defining the problem and seeking the best possible solution is the first step in the innovation process. Ideas may be generated internally; agencies also should examine and perhaps adopt innovations developed in other organizations. One example is the recent "innovation exchange" program between the city of London and New York City. London offers its expertise in dealing with issues like congestion pricing and climate change while New York City shares its experience in improving access to services through 311 and other technology initiatives.

Selection: Which innovations are worth pursuing? This question is particularly important to public sector organizations, which have a hard time defending new ideas and face multiple stakeholders who might say no. The World Bank created an innovative process to give good ideas a fair chance: the Development Marketplace. The Bank set up a "bazaar" in its atrium, with booths allotted to 121 teams, each with an idea to propose. A panel of senior executives from the World Bank, private organizations, and the nonprofit sector evaluated the proposals. In a single day, 11 ideas received funding from a total budget of $3 million.

Implementation: Once selected, an idea must be funded, developed, and executed. Incentive mechanisms such as gainsharing and share-in-savings contracts can help; however, many government programs lack predictable end results. Dealing with uncertainties and unexpected events requires flexibility and willingness to make mid-course corrections. The Florida School Year 2000 Initiative, a school-reform program that provided teachers handheld devices to record student information, worked because officials modified the technology used by the program after they encountered unexpected problems. Successful implementation also requires effective leadership that defines the mission of the organization and builds a coalition for change.

Diffusion: The last stage in the innovation cycle refers to the spread of an innovation throughout an organization or from one organization to another. This requires gaining support from all stakeholders, breaking down organizational silos, and overcoming apathy toward innovations. One way to encourage diffusion is to "create a buzz" around successful innovations. The Florida Department of Children and Families, which provides various child and community care services, slashed customer wait times by 45 minutes, reduced turnover, and saved $11 million annually. After the department's efforts earned several awards, word spread fast, and soon other state and federal agencies copied its efforts.

Part 2:
The five innovation strategies

2 Cultivate

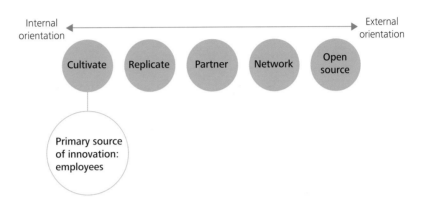

Internal orientation ←————————————————→ External orientation

Cultivate — Replicate — Partner — Network — Open source

Primary source of innovation: employees

There is no established theoretical framework for cultivating innovation — no immutable laws that, when applied, will start good ideas rolling off an assembly line. But successful organizations create an atmosphere that welcomes suggestions — and adopts them when appropriate.

For instance, Southwest Airlines employees spent 10 hours a week for six months brainstorming changes in the company's aircraft operations. Those meetings, which included members of the airline's in-flight, ground, maintenance, and dispatch operations, generated 109 ideas for high-impact changes. A critical part of this process was tapping into the diverse, even if imperfect, knowledge base of each employee. One director from the schedule-planning division successfully challenged assumptions held by the maintenance and dispatch personnel for 30 years.[14] Three ideas developed through these meetings triggered extensive operational adjustments, one of which allowed Southwest to reduce the number of aircraft "swaps" when mechanical failures require one aircraft to be substituted for another.

In the public sector, relatively few organizations encourage change. Instead, stories of successful government innovations often profile determined individuals overcoming formidable odds. Rigid rules and processes, often developed to control corruption and nepotism, constrain innovation. Evidence collected by the NAO report cited earlier is telling: government organizations tend to "accumulate innovations." They generally know what needs to change, but they wait for alterations in "ministerial or policy priorities" or efficiency drives before they implement those changes. Most innovations (around 50 percent) are triggered by senior and middle managers, followed by ministers (around 20 percent).

Frontline employees tend to play a very small part in innovations (around 8 percent), according to the report.[15] They often do not know what constitutes a good suggestion, let alone how to lead an initiative to improve performance. This picture is in sharp contrast to most innovative private sector organizations, which have eschewed hierarchy and created formal structures designed to capture information and feedback from employees.

But it is possible to cultivate an environment in public agencies that more consistently sparks moments of creativity — the brilliant idea, the novel principle, the solution to a long-standing problem, or the argument that finally debunks old prejudices and dogmas. Here's how (figure 2.1):

Tap into the diverse tacit knowledge in the field

Tacit knowledge which exists within the minds of employees, is born of sheer experience. It is the know-how gained by practice and deliberate study, the wisdom and judgment derived from daily exposure to an environment over time. It is the kind of knowledge that makes a 30-year government employee an expert at navigating Byzantine public sector personnel rules.

Tacit knowledge can generate innovation. But how do you capture that knowledge and convert it into practices that not only help organizations perform better but also deliver more valuable service?

Figure 2.1: Cultivate strategy: benefits and approaches

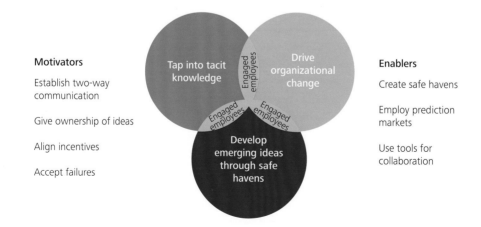

Motivators

Establish two-way communication

Give ownership of ideas

Align incentives

Accept failures

Enablers

Create safe havens

Employ prediction markets

Use tools for collaboration

This question has attracted the attention of the best minds in the business world.

Companies now promote cross-functional excellence, an approach that requires tapping into the divergent perspectives of employees from different functions and disciplines to challenge established mind-sets, open up the organization to new thinking, and generate high-impact solutions.

Frontline employees often know more about customer needs and have better ideas about how to improve performance than their bosses. However, they often need help understanding the needs of the entire organization, explaining how their ideas address those needs, and determining how to implement change.

Engage employees at all levels

Three questions need to be answered when considering how to engage employees to innovate.

How do employees know what a good suggestion is? Tesco, the largest supermarket chain in the United Kingdom, has defined the criteria in simple terms: better for customers, simpler for staff, and cheaper for Tesco. Management communicates these principles to all employees. Each year, the top 2,000 executives spend a week on the shop floor at the checkout counter or in a warehouse stacking shelves. They get feedback from colleagues and customers, collate all the information, and send it to the relevant division heads.[16] The program, called Tesco Week in Store Together (TWIST), is making a real difference in serving customers better by bringing the senior management and store-level employees together. According to Sir Terry Leahy, Tesco's chief executive, "TWIST will mean that every senior manager has worked for a week in store, served our customers, and listened to what they and their colleagues have to say. That is experience you can't get in a training room or on a quick store visit."[17]

Who decides which ideas are worth following up, and who takes charge of implementing changes? The In-House R&D Network at the Bureau of Motor Equipment of the New York City Department of Sanitation allows worksite committees of mechanics to adopt proposals and implement changes within the scope of their operations, with the agreement of the facility manager. Bureau analysts help work out the business case for each project. If the proposal demands greater resources than the operation can provide, or if it requires coordination with other government agencies, the bureau's leaders are enlisted. For even bigger projects, the bureau seeks approval through the city's budget process.[18] A number of innovations by the workers have been patented, such as a device that shuts down the engine to protect it from burnout when the oil in a truck drops too low.[19]

Are frontline employees ready to create the required change? When the U.S. Department of the Interior began a new approach to land management known as "cooperative conservation," it engaged its frontline employees in establishing partnerships to create holistic solutions by combining local understanding with scientific knowledge. For example, to prevent the endangered short-tailed albatrosses from getting caught on the fishermen's hooks in the waters off Alaska, local groups in partnership with scientists came up with several solutions: one of them was to weight the fishing lines to sink the hooks below the surface, where they wouldn't snag the birds.

The department's 4Cs Team, which was formed to identify barriers to and best practices for the new initiative, realized that implementing cooperative conservation required not only technical skills but also managerial capabilities. It further concluded that teams composed of people from diverse professional backgrounds and with varied competencies tend to outperform teams of "experts" who all have the same knowledge and skill sets. For example, the program needed people who could create a work environment that encourages creative thinking, who could persuade others and build consensus, and who would keep up-to-date on key national and international trends. To find such people, the department changed its hiring criteria. It also redesigned its training programs to create the new competencies. To strike a balance between flexibility and accountability, it is currently analyzing exactly how employees can be creative and still meet certain basic policy objectives.

Employ prediction markets

Prediction markets work like stock markets: people make bets on the likely outcome. For example, in the Hollywood Stock Exchange, people use play money to bet on which films will win Oscars in the top eight categories, or how much a film will make in sales.[20]

Research shows that prediction market forecasts routinely outperform opinion polls or expert opinions. That has been the case, for example, with Iowa Electronic Market, which uses real money to predict election results in the United States and elsewhere.[21] Private firms are developing innovative ways to use this principle, creating prediction markets where employees can bet on future events, such as sales forecasts and project end date.

Organizations use this kind of independent mechanism to aggregate diverse insights from their employees. They can then construct a realistic picture of their own operation. For example, Eli Lilly has created an internal market that allows employees to predict which drugs will make it through to the next phase of clinical trials. This gives the company leadership a good sense of which products to put its resources behind.[22] Siemens allows employees to bet on projects they think will finish on time, which helps direct managerial attention to critical projects. Hewlett Packard employs the same mechanism to predict monthly sales of printers more accurately than the marketing team does with its own processes.

Prediction markets could be employed in the public sector to track a number of variables, such as inflation, unemployment, and the likely impact of changes in interest rates on economic activity. Or they could be used internally to identify projects likely to overshoot time and cost estimates. However, to do so, governments will have to liberalize gambling laws that currently restrict the use of prediction markets. Governments are not likely to find the prediction market tool useful for internal projects.

Use tools for collaboration

Web 2.0 is changing the way governments do their business. It makes collaboration possible in innovative ways through blogs, wikis, tags, and peer-to-peer networking.

Blogs or web logs let people share information and knowledge and allow informal networks to operate within an organization. These are "online diaries" of posts and comments that establish a channel of communication and promote free discussion of issues within the organization. Blogs can be updated easily at virtually no cost. They also give management an effective way to convey information to employees, answer questions, build logs of projects, and provide other updates.

Wikis are used to organize and update blogs, but their uses extend beyond that. A wiki is an online tool that allows users to create and edit pages of information, with the changes appearing on the site almost as soon as contributors make them. To control abuse, some systems require users to authenticate their identities before making changes. An example of the use of a wiki in government is Intellipedia, developed by the CIA, which lets employees across a number of security agencies engage in open discussions on topics of concern to them. Typically, a wiki has no structured hierarchy, whether in regard to the names on an organizational chart or the way information might be structured within the site, and no formal control systems for organizing or editing content. These are considered to be the main advantages of a wiki: they give it speed and flexibility.

In addition to wikis, organizations may also use peer-to-peer networking sites (which allow users to share files and data through high-speed connections) for real time collaboration. One of the best-known examples of this technology is the music-sharing service Napster, which music publishers sued successfully for copyright infringement.

The U.S. military is experimenting with peer-to-peer networking to allow troops on the ground to interact and collaborate instantaneously, without being bogged down by organizational and technical protocols and hierarchies.[23] During operations in both Kosovo and Afghanistan, disparate computer systems blocked effective communication between the Army, Navy, and Air Force. Peer-to-peer systems can ease communication among soldiers on the ground and between U.S. troops and allied troops, bypassing the obstacles raised by incompatible systems or security protocols. The most important contribution these collaboration tools make is that they "separate the idea of chain of command from chain of information," according to James Cartwright, vice chairman of the Joint Chiefs of Staff.[24]

Tap informal networks

Recent research shows that informal channels are more efficient conduits for information and ideas than formal channels defined by the organizational structure. The methodology and process of social network analysis is a good example of a new means of igniting organizational learning. As noted by experts Dr. Rob Cross of the University of Virginia and Valdis Krebs, management consultant, social network analysis of an organization or community's informal networks can provide new insights for leaders trying to understand how organizations work.

Dr. Cross has argued that social network analysis can be a valuable analytical tool for exposing and analyzing networks that exist within an agency or community. Social network analysis can help to answer important questions, including:

- How does information flow across networks?
- Are certain people overly central to managing work and information flows?
- Are some people loosely connected and underused?
- Are there divisive subgroups?
- Is the network's level of connection sufficient?

Consider the need for interagency cooperation for national security. The ability to create and maintain a personal network is crucial to enhancing collaboration and transcending the bureaucracy that has historically blocked interorganizational cooperation. As such, security agencies could greatly enhance their self-awareness, and fill an important information gap, by using social network analysis to increase their understanding of actual processes and workflows.

Dr. Cross's social network analysis tool also reveals the most important players in an agency or communities' informal networks, including those who facilitate and impede collaboration. This kind of analysis has the potential to be a baseline study from which to assess progress on collaboration. It also could fill a key

knowledge gap by giving an accurate portrayal of the agency's current level of connectivity and integration. Finally, the analysis can identify key niche experts who have abilities that may be very specific to certain areas of the network. Productive peripheral positions can be created for these individuals, along with individualized career paths that fit their specialized skill set.

Tapping into the wisdom of employees requires new mechanisms that separate responsibility and performance from job title and position in the hierarchy. However, organizations need to supplement these efforts with incentive mechanisms that nurture change by breaking the perception that innovations are high-risk, low-gain affairs.

Drive organizational change

Creating an innovative organization does not always require large-scale changes that turn the organization upside down. Sometimes it merely requires figuring out the levers for change. Like the trim tab that turns the rudder, changing the direction of a huge ship, these levers of an organization facilitate change without a major upheaval.

Small changes can sometimes create big results. Using blogs and wikis, creating prediction markets, and allowing employees to implement their own ideas: these are small changes to create big results. It does not stop there, however. Creating an innovative organization requires addressing issues that influence behavior. For instance, when employees are asked to share their views openly, are managers ready to get honest feedback that shows what is wrong? Or will they get embroiled in a blame game, trying to corner the employee into thinking that she is wrong?

Take a "systems" view

For a ship to turn left, its rudder has to turn right. For the rudder to turn right, the trim tab (like a tiny rudder, which helps turn the rudder around.)[25] has to go left. A captain knowing the way the whole system works together prevents the ship from going off-course. A systemic view allows an understanding of the interrelationship between key variables and how changing a variable affects the entire system. Human systems are, of course, infinitely more complex than rudders.[26]

Systems influence behavior. If you create a system where employees generate a lot of good ideas but fail to put in place measures to acknowledge and implement these ideas, it will ultimately create a negative response that brings the entire system back into balance. In this case, the idea generation process will slow to a crawl. The harder you push the system to generate ideas, the greater the resistance because more good ideas accumulate and employees get the signal that their ideas are not being heard. Addressing this systemic problem requires building credibility by tracking the conversion rate of good ideas into meaningful innovations and converting more and more good ideas into practice.

Align incentives

Governments need to provide incentives for risk taking and create mechanisms for calculating risk, so that the fear of failure does not trump the desire to create new initiatives. Any innovation carries risks; in general, the bigger the change, the higher the risk (see inset on "Types of Risk"). Public scrutiny and media cynicism make it dangerous for public employees to launch any sort of new initiative except the kind that is virtually guaranteed to succeed. After all, no public manager wants to drink her morning glass of orange juice reading a headline in 12-point type describing her latest screw-up.[27]

Many governments provide financial rewards (bonuses and performance pay) and offer awards and recognition to innovators.[28] Gainsharing, or sharing the financial benefits of performance improvement and cost reduction with employees, is one example of this.

The U.S. federal government has developed rules and programs meant to recognize the value of contributions that employees make to the government. However, "those of us with government experience," notes Patrick J. Keogh, "know that award programs tend to be reactive rather than proactive."[29] Keogh, a onetime employee at Vice President Al Gore's National Performance Review, cites an interesting personal example to show that these programs are not as well publicized or utilized as they should be. While working at the General Services Administration (GSA), Keogh was approached by an investment banker with a proposal that would save the government $25 million. Keogh realized that he would need the support of six or seven key people within the government for the initiative to succeed.

TSA's idea factory

In April 2007, the U.S. Transportation Security Administration (TSA) launched a secure intranet Web site called the "Idea Factory" that allows employees to submit ideas for improving agency operations and processes. By the end of January 2009, employees had submitted 7,837 ideas and 69,712 comments. Of those ideas, about 39 have been implemented by the TSA.

The TSA created the Idea Factory site after an internal survey revealed that TSA employees believed their voices were not being heard by the agency's leadership. TSA employees now review ideas posted on the site, and they vote for the suggestions they think are most worthy of management attention. The best ideas receive a certificate and a memento from the organization.

Response to the TSA's Idea Factory has sparked widespread interest in the idea as a method for breaking through organizational barriers to innovation. The site is an extremely good example of how to create a positive environment for innovative ideas.

The guiding principle for any initiative to generate innovations is to understand that ultimately you will get only as many ideas as you have the ability to implement. A purely linear view of the Idea Factory process would suggest that because employees submitted so many good ideas, they translated into multiple initiatives. However, a systems view would suggest that so many good ideas were submitted because these ideas were acknowledged and implemented, creating a positive environment for submitting more ideas.

Types of risk

• **Organizational:** Costs of introducing change could turn out to be higher than the benefits.

• **Political:** Politicians and senior officials do not want to be seen backing the wrong horse — or a losing one.

• **Personal:** Failure could damage the career of the person introducing the change. Success,

on the other hand, may do little to advance career growth.

• **Counter-reinvention:** The value of an innovation can be offset by new rules and regulations. For example, the death knell for factory assembly of complete homes was sounded by new building regulations (tougher zoning and land-use ordinances, wheelchair access for multifamily homes, and prohibition of lead paint) that made this kind of new housing prohibitively expensive.

Researching the Code of Federal Regulations and GSA's internal orders, he found a provision buried in the personnel policy that allowed cash awards to employees who created savings. He decided that he could share the award with his colleagues as an incentive for pushing ahead with the project. "A year later, the deal was done and we requested our spiff," Keogh says. "It was split between five GSA employees and two at the treasury department."[30]

Keogh points out that many government agencies have the same kinds of award and bonus programs found in the private sector. Managers do not use them widely, however, and employees often have no idea how they are likely to be measured and rewarded if they make suggestions that improve operations.

Proactive award programs empower employees to pursue rewards, rather than leaving managers to dispense them as an afterthought for a job well done. Aligning incentives also

means that when employees perform in ways that merit awards, their annual reviews note that performance. Cultural change is not likely to happen if employees who "risk" innovation see no positive impact on their careers.

Some organizations also provide innovative employees with grants they can use in any way to promote further innovation, perhaps hiring staff or procuring new technology. In government, this tactic sometimes takes the form of a productivity bank, a pot of money that funds good ideas offered by employees, thus encouraging employees to suggest new ideas and receive funding.

Accept failures

Innovation is about experimentation. Experiments often fail. A can't-afford-to-fail environment is not very conducive to making ambitious decisions or investments. It also seldom results in a high-performance organization.

Successful innovations tend to be unpredictable. Innovative companies often build failure into their systems of innovation. The idea is to fail quickly if you have to, learn from the experience, and move on to the next big idea. At IDEO, the design company that designed Apple's first mouse and the sleek palm-held device called Palm V, the culture invites employees to "have the guts to create a straw man" that others can criticize, so that they can "fail often to succeed sooner."[31] 3M, which manufactures adhesives, oral care products, and software for supply chain management, among other things, brings together "skunk works" teams (discussed in the next section) to investigate the problems in a potential product.

Accepting failures has the potential to keep good money from following bad money. If employees know that they can stop a project that has failed or is likely to fail without damaging their careers, they are more likely to shut it down before it blows up into a big-ticket failure.[32] The option to do so is better than persisting with a project to the end, wasting time, money, and effort. Accepting failure also sends the signal to employees that innovation is important and that failure will not result in a blame game.

Develop and nurture emerging ideas

Bureaucratic structures developed to enforce compliance with rules and procedures can kill budding ideas because innovations often require challenging the status quo or questioning long-held assumptions that may have worked well in the past. Without loosening the sometimes suffocating grip of bureaucracy over the more creative employees, it will be difficult to motivate them to innovate. This means dismantling or bypassing structures and systems that ensure conformity and stifle creativity, and building new structures that encourage fresh thinking. One such structure is the safe haven.

Safe havens — separate units kept close to mainstream activities but away from line organizations — permit low-risk experimentation. For example, New York's Center for Technology in Government (CTG) lets state and local agencies experiment with computer-based processes before making big investments.[33] The state's Office of Children and Family Services recently collaborated with CTG on a pilot to evaluate whether portable IT platforms, such as wireless laptops, could improve child protective service investigations while reducing costs.

The pilot ran in two counties, Westchester and Monroe, and a detailed assessment was made based on surveys, interviews, and analysis of data from the central case management database. The results showed that mobile devices improved performance. But the analysis also revealed a number of qualifiers, such as the need to account for individual work preferences and organizational support. The focus now is on conducting a second phase of larger-scale trials before full deployment.[34]

Conducting pilots like these in a safe haven gives employees time to develop emerging ideas and protects them from short-term budget constraints and premature criticism. While safe havens work as enablers in the

42

public sector, they can also work as motivators for "renegade" thinkers — not people seeking to undermine authority, but independent visionaries looking to achieve results. Not content merely to acquiesce and conform, these talented individuals can find working in small teams with little bureaucracy and paperwork an exhilarating and rewarding experience.

Skunk works

A type of safe haven, skunk works are composed of a small group of highly talented and motivated people who are freed from bureaucracy, paper work, and most routine administrative responsibilities. The term originated in 1943 at the Lockheed Aircraft Corporation, where a small group that went by that name delivered the prototype XP-80 fighter plane in 143 days, seven days ahead of schedule. Skunk works have the potential to deliver results in governments as well. Some of the best examples of skunk works in the public sector are the ones formed to attack the most complex problems.

The Manhattan Project, the program to develop the nuclear bomb during World War II, can be considered a scaled-up version of a skunk works project. Relocated to New Mexico with their families, some of the finest scientific minds of that time put together the formulas for refining uranium and created a working atom bomb within six years, well ahead of their German counterparts.

The Technology Strategy Board within the UK Department for Business Enterprise and Regulatory Reform is a more recent example of skunk works in the public sector. A small group of people from diverse backgrounds (business, government, and academia) is charged with translating knowledge into innovation, setting priorities for research and funding, and developing the government's strategy for establishing the United Kingdom as a global leader in innovation and technology. For example, it has set up the Low Impact Buildings Innovation Platform that will bring together key players from industry, academia, and government to reduce carbon emissions from buildings. (Forty-five percent of the total carbon emission in the United Kingdom comes from buildings.) Efforts directed at meeting the target of a 60 percent reduction in carbon emission by 2050 will likely prove futile unless there is dramatic improvement in the design, construction, and management of buildings. The initiative will commission studies, set up demonstrator projects to validate solutions, and explore new business models, among other things, with financial support from the board and other funding agencies.

Intrapreneurs

The American Heritage Dictionary defines an intrapreneur as "a person within a large corporation who takes direct responsibility for turning an idea into a profitable finished product through assertive risk-taking and innovation." Gifford Pinchot, an author and consultant on innovation management, introduced the concept in his 1985 book, *Intrapreneuring*. His goal: to show how large organizations can foster innovations.[35] The idea is gaining currency

SHARP minds tackle tough problems

Each summer for the past three years, diverse groups of government and private sector experts have gathered in secluded and classified locations to tackle some of America's most difficult intelligence challenges. These experts spend a month together examining critical issues through the annual Summer Hard Problem (SHARP) program, sponsored by the federal U.S. Office of the Deputy Director of National Intelligence for Analysis.

This year, the SHARP program focused on two issues: potential intelligence uses for computer-based virtual worlds such as Second Life, and how to slow the worldwide growth of extremism. These intensive four-week programs are designed to reduce "groupthink" within the notoriously insular intelligence community by fostering interaction between government officials and outside experts. The extremism session, for instance, brought together authorities on anthropology, social psychology, insurgency, and Islamic thought.

The SHARP program's goal is to identify novel approaches and forge relationships that lead to ongoing collaboration on vital issues of national security. The program is patterned after a long-running and highly successful project by the National Security Agency, which enlists top mathematicians to work on sophisticated encryption issues.

---

in various ways in the business world. Pioneering companies such as Google and 3M allow their employees to spend close to 20 percent of their time developing their own business ideas. 3M made one of its big breakthroughs, Post-it notes, thanks to an intrapreneur who wanted something to mark pages in his hymn book.

But intrapreneuring isn't confined to the private sector. When budget cuts in the 1990s threatened administrative functions at the U.S. Forest Service, the agency created self-supporting business units that deliver a wide range of services to forest managers. Now internal Forest Service "intraprises" handle tasks like estimating lumber yields and measuring the environmental impact of land improvement projects for other Forest Service units, and they charge fees that cover all their expenses, including overhead costs, salaries, and benefits.

The idea, now known as the Enterprise Program, wasn't imposed from above. Instead it emerged from both ends of the organization. When David Radloff, chief of the Forest Service's reinvention efforts, challenged employees to make the organization more self-supporting, the agency's Pacific Southwest region led the way. The region's financial manager, Mike Duffey, contacted Pinchot and ultimately created internal units that now compete for agency tasks much like outside businesses would.

Creating these enterprises within the Forest Service wasn't easy. It took a leap of faith for government employees to substitute entrepreneurship for secure government jobs. Basic business systems weren't in place, and employees had to be taught to write business plans, create presentations, and handle spreadsheets. In addition, others within the Forest Service resisted the initiative, fearing the enterprises could jeopardize their jobs.

Despite these early challenges, the Enterprise Program became "a glorious success," says Pinchot. "It was handicapped. It fought with one hand behind its back [against] accounting systems that didn't support it, human resource systems that didn't support it," he said. "And it is still delivering exceptional service [to] happy customers who love using the same Enterprise Teams over and over again."[36]

The program's 13 enterprise units collected $27 million in 2006, a modest sum compared with the Forest Service budget, but a significant increase from $200,000 at the start of the initiative.

Cultivating innovation is an evolutionary process; it cannot be done overnight. It involves trial and error, experimentation without taking undue risk, and adaptation to change. Conducted wisely, an effort to encourage innovation also involves keeping in touch with other innovators. That will help governments quickly replicate successful innovations by adapting them to the local context instead of trying to reinvent the wheel every time they seek to do something new. How to do this well is the subject of the next chapter.

Chapter in a box

The cultivate strategy involves engaging employees at all levels with diverse sets of skills to generate ideas and see them through to final execution. The strategy enables governments to realize the following benefits:

Tap into diverse knowledge in the field. Embedded knowledge is born of sheer experience but how do you capture that knowledge and convert it into practices that not only help organizations perform better but also deliver more valuable service? Governments can tap into the tacit knowledge in the field by utilizing these approaches:

Engage employees at all levels. The R&D Network at the Bureau of Motor Equipment of the New York City Department of Sanitation allows worksite committees of mechanics to adopt proposals and implement changes within the scope of their operations, with the agreement of the facility manager.

Employ prediction markets. Organizations use this kind of independent mechanism to aggregate diverse insights from its employees. Siemens allows employees to bet on projects they think will finish on time, which helps direct managerial attention to critical projects.

Use collaboration tools. Web 2.0 collaboration tools such as blogs, wikis, tags, and peer-to-peer networking can facilitate bottom-up innovation by giving front-line employees an opportunity to float their ideas directly to peers and senior management.

Tap informal markets. The social network analysis tool reveals the most important players in an agency or communities' informal networks. It can help increase cooperation and collaboration through increased understanding of actual processes and workflows.

Drive organizational change. Understand the system to identify levers that create big results and influence behavior. Governments can encourage innovation and drive organizational change by:

Taking a "systems" view. A systemic view allows an understanding of the interrelationship between key variables and how changing one variable can affect the entire system.

Aligning incentives. Many governments allow cash awards to employees who create savings. The key is for managers to use these incentives proactively.

Accepting failures. A can't-afford-to-fail environment is not conducive to making ambitious decisions or creating a high-performance organization. IDEO, a design consultancy, invites employees to create prototypes that can be criticized by others so that employees fail often to succeed sooner.

Develop emerging ideas through safe havens. Developing big, bold ideas in-house often requires dismantling or bypassing structures and systems that ensure conformity and stifle creativity. One way of doing this is to create safe havens that are separate units kept close to mainstream activities but away from the line organization. *Skunk works* is a type of safe haven in which a small group of highly talented and motivated people are freed from bureaucracy, paper work, and most routine administrative responsibilities.

The cultivate strategy works best when:
- The organization believes in the importance of sustained innovation
- Innovation is needed to improve a core function of the organization
- Core customers are affected
- Adherence to processes and enforced uniformity blocks performance
- There is a trade-off between centralized control and innovation
- Innovation requires a unique understanding of the public sector environment
- It is part of cultural change
- Risks cannot be shared or transferred
- Privacy and security are big concerns.

3 Replicate

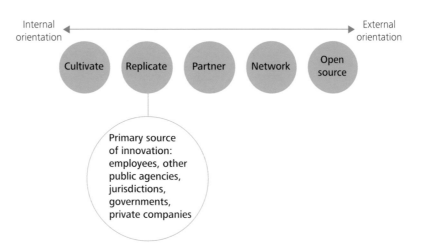

Internal orientation ←———————————→ External orientation

Cultivate | Replicate | Partner | Network | Open source

Primary source of innovation: employees, other public agencies, jurisdictions, governments, private companies

The public policy process offers any number of opportunities for crushing innovation. New ideas can be destroyed in the design phase, they can fail to make it to law, or they can be botched during implementation. And, of course, sometimes seemingly good ideas prove faulty when put into practice.

For all of these reasons, one of the best public sector innovation strategies is to borrow proven ideas from other governments. An idea can be argued ad nauseam in theory, but it is difficult to argue with results.

The replicate strategy is about public agencies creating systems to identify and adopt innovations from elsewhere. But replicating good ideas in government has often proved difficult. As Bill Clinton said during his presidency: "Nearly every problem has been solved by someone, somewhere. The frustration is that we can't seem to replicate [those solutions] anywhere else."[37] President Clinton spoke from experience. His promise of creating at least 100 clones of Chicago's South Shore Bank, which attracts savings to be invested in economically weak neighborhoods underserved by traditional banks, ultimately did not come to fruition.[38]

To replicate good ideas you first need to spot them. Driven by competitive pressure, private firms have a strong incentive to track what other firms are doing and to use that intelligence to produce better products. Government agencies lack that built-in incentive, so they need to create structured

"I've been stealing everyone's ideas for 15 years and putting them all together. We developed an approach that's working at a time when people are desperate for nonconventional answers."[39]

Stephen Goldsmith, the former mayor of

Indianapolis and currently faculty director of the

Innovations in American Government Program

at Harvard's Kennedy School of Government.

methods for discovering and adopting innovations from other jurisdictions.

But merely finding ideas is not enough. Replication may fail when the innovation does not fit the local context. The Chicago South Shore Bank program, for example, ran into resistance in communities that preferred local credit unions. Many innovations spring up locally to meet local requirements. Variations in political, judicial, and cultural context can stymie the spread of innovations. When the contexts differ widely, innovations that work well in one jurisdiction simply do not apply to others.[40]

Even when an innovation is a good fit for a local context, multiple factors may inhibit its successful implementation. The Indianapo-

lis "competition and costing" model, which allowed city employees to compete with the private sector to provide certain public services, is a good example of an innovation that required customization to local context. The idea of public-private competition had been around for some time when Mayor Goldsmith began to promote its adoption. For example, the city of Phoenix, Arizona, had begun competitive bidding for refuse collection, landscape management, and street repair in 1979, long before Goldsmith became the mayor of Indianapolis in 1991. Indianapolis had to go through its own process of tailoring public-private competition before trying the idea (discussed in more detail later in the chapter).

Challenges to replication

Serendipity in adoption of innovations: Good ideas often spread through external sources, such as policy entrepreneurs or award programs. The lack of structured processes for finding and implementing new ideas results in a great deal of chance in the adoption of innovations.

Local resistance to new ideas: The "not invented here" syndrome can hinder adoption of innovations from other jurisdictions, especially if there were failures in the past. This resistance can lead employees to make surface changes without bothering to implement the necessary underlying systemic reforms.

Lack of incentives to spread innovation: Agencies and employees that spawn innovations often do little to spread their ideas or articulate what made them successful. They see their role end with the implementation of the innovation.

Figure 3.1: Replication strategy: benefits and approaches

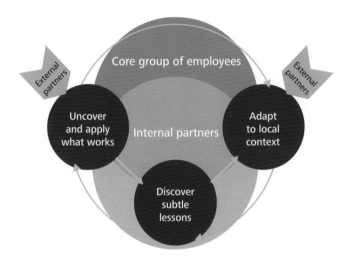

Certain kinds of innovations, particularly in the area of social welfare, are more difficult to replicate. With these kinds of programs, the relation between cause and effect often is not clear, adoption can be costly, and subtle factors such as motivation prove difficult to measure. This is where cooperation among public sector agencies can help. The subtle factors that made the innovation successful can be passed on by the designers to the potential adopters of the innovation.

The idea of replication is also based on the notion that governments often have similar needs and common means for meeting them at their disposal. This realization opens the possibility of collaborating with other public agencies to spread innovations from one jurisdiction to the next. A program such as Missouri's Parents as Teachers initiative, in which counselors teach the principles of child development to the parents of very young children, is likely to be a perfect candidate to spread through cooperation. The problem (in this case, lack of parental knowledge) is likely to be common for governments, and sharing the solution (educating parents) has no competitive implications.

Replication strategies must therefore take into account the specific issues associated with replication in the public sector and be flexible enough to ensure successful implementation (figure 3.1). The replication strategy enables governments to:

- **Uncover and apply what works.** If others have managed to experiment

"We borrowed and adapted several ideas from other states and cities during my tenure as governor. It worked well because we could see what worked elsewhere and why, and then tailor and deploy those best practices in a way that fit our state's unique needs and circumstances."

Former Pennsylvania Governor Tom Ridge

with a good idea and it is seen to work, it increases the likelihood of gaining acceptance for the idea. Further, these ideas are not as risky as others that have not been implemented yet

- **Adapt innovations to local context.** Just because an idea worked in some context does not mean it can be implemented as is. The idea still needs to be adapted to the local context where it can run into a hostile environment

- **Discover subtle lessons.** It is important that the subtle lessons in implementing an idea are passed on to would-be innovators and the way to do it is to understand how ideas spread in the public sector.

Uncover and apply what works

The best way to avoid reinventing the wheel is to make sure that when someone else invents something, you get the news and, ideally, a copy of the plans. Governments with ongoing programs to learn about innovations and best practices developed elsewhere amass a rich storehouse of ideas they can adapt to their own needs.

Governments need some kind of structured way of discovering and tracking innovations and best practices. The oldest program of this kind is the Texas Performance Review, created in 1992. Every two years, this program looks far and wide for innovations Texas can apply to its own government to cut costs, increase public value, and improve performance. The Texas Performance Review typically has a team of 12–24 specialists who conduct an extensive review of Texas agencies' performance and compare it to best practices around the world. The team selects ideas that hold the most promise for further development and customization to the local context. Innovations that are easy to implement often receive high priority, as do programs that reduce costs and increase revenue, elicit voluntary participation, or do not require more expertise or time than is available.[41]

The criteria that Texas Performance Review lists for replication point to one single theme: the ability of the adopter to implement the innovation. Biting off more than the organization can chew is sure to result in failure. For example, experts usually are needed when it comes to replicating innovations, but the organization needs to be sure that its frontline employees have the ability to implement the innovation. Replication, therefore, entails selecting those ideas that the organization can execute now or else building the required competencies within the organization.

Take the New York City CompStat program, which won the Innovations in American Government Award in 1996. CompStat helped cut the crime rate in New York City dramatically and has been replicated widely across cities in the United States. This program uses crime statistics to determine how to deploy resources and measures the effect of each individual intervention to refine deployment further. The idea of using statistics to drive resource allocation is simple and intuitive, and it does not take extraordinary resources to build the

Figure 3.2: Adapting an innovation to the local context

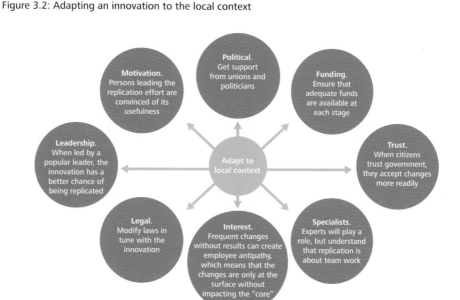

required infrastructure (analysts, office space, computers, conference room, and the like).

But efforts to replicate CompStat elsewhere haven't always been successful. A key feature of the program is to regularly analyze gains and failures. The goal is to track the impact of new programs, single out approaches that are working and replace ineffective practices with new tactics. However, CompStat's metrics constantly evolve to suit changing conditions, and they must be customized to local requirements. In one jurisdiction, the shrinking number of weapons confiscated by officers was taken as a sign that a program to remove

illegal guns from the streets wasn't working. In fact, the program was so successful that there were simply fewer illegal weapons to confiscate. This example has a clear message: metrics used to evaluate a program continually need to be re-examined. The broader implication for replication is that even relatively simple and intuitive ideas like using statistics to deploy resources must be tailored to local needs.

Adapt to local context

Applying a blueprint from elsewhere without considering the local situation or stage of

311: when government innovation succeeds

Imagine buying an expensive item online only to find when it arrives at your home that it's not working properly. You call customer service and get stuck in automated customer service — going through a series of confusing voice prompts and pressing various numbers with the likelihood that when you finally get through to a live person, you're transferred to another department where you find yourself talking to a machine once again.

Contrast this situation with what happens at one innovative organization. First, there is a single, well-known number to call for any complaint or question related to any of its myriad businesses, and every caller reaches a real live person within 10 seconds of placing the call. Moreover, the customer service representatives are so well trained that 85 percent of the time your issue can be addressed by the person who takes your call. No perilous call transfers; no exile to an automated system.

Moments after you hang up the phone you receive an email acknowledging your call, specifying how it will be resolved, and giving you a tracking number. With the tracking number, you can go online anytime and see if your issue has been fixed, and if not, you can see who is working on your complaint. A few days later you get a follow-up letter from the CEO. This is the Rolls Royce of customer service.

But it's not Rolls Royce. It is government behaving — well. The innovative service is called "311," and it started in Baltimore and soon spread to Chicago, New York City, Barcelona, Tokyo, and dozens of other cities around the world. In these cities, whether you want to file a complaint, request a trash pickup, or even inquire whether an upcoming parade is going to shut down your street, you dial "311" and within 10 seconds you'll be getting all the assistance you need. Thanks to a highly sophisticated customer-relationship-management software system, your issue will be distributed to the appropriate agency, logged, tracked, and monitored. In the end, you'll get a letter from the mayor making sure you were satisfied with the results.

In New York City, 311 has made it easier for residents to report quality-of-life issues. Excessive noise inspections are up 94 percent and rodent exterminations have increased by more than a third. And since the Building Department now uses 311 to streamline its permit review process, the wait time for builders to get an appointment with an inspector has plummeted from more than a month to under a week.

Today, not only does the 311 system put all of a city's services within easy, round-the-clock reach of residents, but city officials can use the millions of data points they collect each month to make better resource

decisions, spotting trends that they otherwise may have missed. Case in point: New York City's chronic Sunday morning parking problem. Before 311, officials didn't realize there was a big problem since calls were placed to numerous places (police precincts, city agencies, etc.). After the 311 system was implemented, parking complaints all went into a centralized system. Once officials had all the data in a single place, they could mine it and see they had a chronic problem, namely that churchgoers are habitual parking violators, infuriating their fellow New Yorkers who reside in the vicinity of the city's more than 1,000 churches. Parking complaints are now geocoded and routed directly to the nearest police precinct's computer so they can be handled more expeditiously.

Through the savvy use of 311 systems, cities have been able to tap into the collective wisdom of their residents and businesses to better understand their needs and thereby allow government officials to catch problems before they reach the crisis stage. In essence, mayors can tap into a hitherto unused asset — the eyes and ears of millions of their residents — to better diagnose problems and manage the city's business.

development can be a recipe for disaster. For example, most civil service reform initiatives in Africa that have tried to reproduce institutions from the developed world have failed.[42] Merely copying an innovation rarely delivers the right results. It has to be adapted to the local context (figure 3.2). Government needs to align the innovation with the goals and capabilities of the local jurisdiction and also overcome legal, institutional, and ideological hurdles.

As mentioned earlier, one innovation widely replicated across jurisdictions is public-private competition to deliver a given service. The idea is to provide public employees a fair chance to retain their jobs when public services are let out for competition while promoting efficiency and customer focus. Though the idea of introducing public-private competition appears simple and attractive, its implementation requires extensive research into best practices, clearly defined performance criteria, regulatory changes, and systems to measure costs in the public sector. To make public agencies flexible enough to withstand competition from the private sector, the government of Georgia reviewed 1,600 regulations, eliminating nearly 27 percent of these, and amending another 40 percent. Until the city of Indianapolis hired an accounting firm to develop an activity-based model of accounting for costs, city officials had no idea that the cost of snow plowing, for instance, varied from $117 a mile to around $40 a mile in different parts of the city. Without a proper accounting system, public employees would not have been able to assess

their costs and submit a winning proposal.

Charismatic but pragmatic leadership also plays a critical role in successful replication. This is where Mayor Goldsmith was particularly successful. He had the support of citizens and voters, but he also managed to gain the support of frontline employees. This at times required making tough decisions. For example, when employees suggested removing some middle management positions to cut costs, Goldsmith backed them. He also worked to provide technical and business support to frontline employees.

Replicating an idea from one locality to another local context also requires managing stakeholders who want to preserve the status quo. In 1978, in response to Deng Xiaoping's new aphorism "to get rich is glorious," several local cadres in a small village in east China secretly got together to split farming land across households and privatize the right to use and derive profit from it. When they learned what the farmers were doing, however, party leaders objected. Deng intervened, prevailing on the party leadership to legalize and approve the initiative, actively promote the replication of the model, and accept the replacement of people's communes by village governments. The results of this experiment were documented and paved the way for the Household Production Responsibility System. By 1984 this family-based model covered 99 percent of Chinese villages; agricultural output increased by 8.2 percent annually from 1980 to 1985, with half of the increase attributed to growth in productivity.[43]

Discover subtle lessons

In the public sector, regional diffusion occurs when agencies adopt innovations from their sister agencies in neighboring states.[44] It is often easier to reach out to neighboring jurisdictions to understand what made the innovation successful because government employees are more likely to know their counterparts in the contiguous districts, regions, or states.

Thus one way to speed diffusion of ideas and innovations is to build relationships with other government agencies using all available channels of communication. This practice is in line with the idea of diffusion through interlocking networks, such as the diffusion of "poison pills" (strategies designed to prevent takeover bids) in the private sector through directors who serve on multiple boards.[45]

A "relationship network" — developed through communities of practice (both online and offline), the efforts of well-connected "policy entrepreneurs," or less formal channels such as lunch meetings — can help governments identify good ideas as well as the key people who can help with replication. What is often quite effective are "communities of practice" (CoPs): self-organizing social groups formed by people working in the same field to share experiential knowledge, discuss problems, create solutions, and build innovations. Their purpose is to gain the tacit knowledge residing in other parts of the organization or in distinct organizations. This network becomes essential when rapid external change necessitates creation of a learning organization. CoPs are also efficient conduits of explicit knowledge as people prefer to ask a colleague rather than go through a manual on the topic, cutting the time needed to solve a problem.

Communities of practice could become very effective tools for organizations that are likely to see a vast store of knowledge walk out the door as the baby boomers begin to retire. Years of experience give practitioners an intuitive grasp of their subject matter, the ability to handle exceptions, and the facility to think through alternatives. This is the kind of knowledge that helps them make snap judgments or "thin-slice," to use the term coined by Malcolm Gladwell in his book *Blink: The Power of Thinking Without Thinking*.[46] The problem with this kind of knowledge is we often cannot tell exactly how we know what we know. Ask a tennis pro how she knows when to hit the ball and the answer would likely be: through years of practice. Starting a community of practice where experts think aloud about problems raised by less experienced employees can be a great way of passing on this intuitive knowledge and replicating success stories.

Collaboration ensures that governments pass along the subtle lessons they learn from each experiment with innovation. To formalize the process of collaborative replication, the city of Miami has established a national committee to take its Community Partnership for Homeless program, an innovative outreach initiative for helping the homeless, to the national level. Representatives from other cities can use this committee as a resource to replicate the "Miami Plan."[47]

It can take decades for information about an innovation to spread from one part of the government to another. Awards programs, such as the Innovation in American Government Awards program, were created to speed up this process. The three-step process for replicating innovations that involves identifying innovations, adapting them to the local context, and collaborating to spread them is likely to ease and speed up replication. The principle behind the strategy of replication is to move from copying successful innovations randomly to establishing processes that actively manage and disseminate innovations. Seen this way, adopting the replication strategy forms an essential component of creating a learning organization and any investments made to create structures for identifying and adapting innovations are likely to offer big returns. This has been the case with the Texas Performance Review, which has saved the state of Texas billions of dollars over the years.

60

Chapter in a box

The replicate strategy suggests that governments can build on existing innovations elsewhere in new contexts. The replicate strategy allows governments to realize the following benefits:

Uncover and apply what works. Benchmark innovations others have already implemented. Every two years the Texas Performance Review searches for innovations that Texas can apply to its own government to cut costs, increase public value, and improve performance. The program has saved Texas billions of dollars since 1992.

Adapt to local context. Align innovation with the goals and capabilities of the local jurisdiction and be aware of regional legal, institutional, and ideological hurdles. Before launching innovations, understand best practices, define performance criteria, develop metrics, and research regulatory barriers.

Discover subtle lessons. Reach out to neighboring jurisdictions and other government agencies to understand what made the innovation successful. Communities of practice — self-organizing social groups formed by people working in the same field — can be catalysts for innovation sharing.

The replication strategy works best when:
- Discovery costs are high
- The innovation has a proven track record in multiple jurisdictions elsewhere
- The innovation is highly transferable
- The idea is simple and easily understood
- Cause-and-effect relationships are clear.

4 Partner

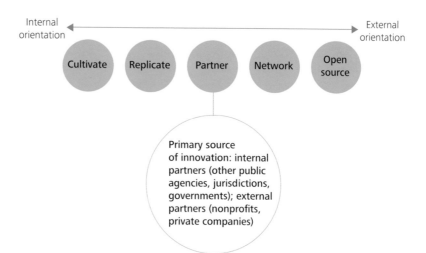

Internal orientation ← → External orientation

Cultivate · Replicate · **Partner** · Network · Open source

Primary source of innovation: internal partners (other public agencies, jurisdictions, governments); external partners (nonprofits, private companies)

Many of today's problems are so complex that no single agency can solve them. Tasks such as reducing poverty, improving health care, or fighting terrorism simply demand more resources — and more innovative thinking — than one organization can bring to bear. The need for both new resources and new thinking drives growing interest in partnering among government agencies, and among government, private industry, universities, and nonprofits.

These relationships let governments test new ideas quickly by importing them from innovative partners. They also help agencies overcome bureaucratic and financial constraints, allowing them to attack long-standing problems with novel methods and cutting edge technologies.

For example, the United Nations Foundation and the Vodafone Group Foundation launched a $30 million technology partnership in 2005 to develop mobile technology for responding to emergencies and collecting health data. Working with a nonprofit consultancy, the partnership created EpiSurveyor, the first free, open-source software for collecting health data. EpiSurveyor eliminates paper forms traditionally used to gather health data. Instead, health researchers collect data in the field using handheld computing devices and transfer the information to desktop computers for processing and analysis. The inexpensive and user-friendly software makes data collection easy and information analysis faster. Further, the new process cuts the cost of program assessments, which typically account for 10 percent of project expenses. Combining the UN's grasp of the issue with Vodafone's technology expertise and resources resulted in innovation that streamlines the collection of health data and reduces cost. Partnerships such as this are gaining popularity throughout the public sector.

There is also a growing interest in public-public partnerships to develop holistic solutions to complex problems. For instance, British Columbia (Canada), Washington, California, Oregon, and Alaska recently announced the Pacific Coast Collaborative agreement to foster innovation, research, and development. "One state alone cannot solve the fight against climate change, or protect our entire ocean, or clean the air we all share — but together, we have the tremendous power to protect our environment," said California Governor Arnold Schwarzenegger.[48]

Besides the sheer complexity of problems and the need to find new financial resources, several other factors drive governments to seek innovation through partnering strategies.

Demand for more personalized services. Citizens are accustomed to the convenience and personalization offered by private sector services. Multiple commercial services are available at single locations and products are delivered quickly to buyers' doorsteps. Now citizens want the same level of service from government. They demand access to personalized home-based health care or low-cost public transport, delivered to them through multiple channels. Meeting these expectations can be daunting for public agencies

alone, but achievable with the right partners.

Need for increased efficiency. Partnerships can help agencies overcome internal barriers to efficiency. For instance, managerial flexibility and performance-based systems boost efficiency. But balancing flexibility with accountability has proven challenging for public agencies. Using partners lets agencies acquire the skills, knowledge, and managerial acumen needed to implement these new techniques.

Desire to manage risk. Efforts to improve performance and meet citizen expectations require new and innovative approaches, yet the public sector environment remains mired in the fear of failure and wary of funding untested approaches. This means that agencies may need to join with partners willing to share and minimize the perceived risks.

The partnership innovation model can enable governments to address these issues and to realize the following benefits (figure 4.1):

- Seek new solutions
- Test new approaches
- Overcome internal constraints
- Benefit from cross-border diffusion.

Seek out new solutions

Partnerships let government agencies import innovations from best-in-class organizations, essentially allowing agencies to add new strengths to their existing expertise. Working with public or private partners also enables agencies to deliver more comprehensive, and usually more efficient, solutions.

Figure 4.1: Partnership-driven innovation strategy: benefits and approaches

Focus on customers

Companies that have mastered the art of innovation to meet customer needs can lend their expertise to public sector agencies through partnerships. Citizens want government to match the convenience of private sector services. Increasingly, they expect personalized access to government services 24x7, through multiple channels. But governments often cannot meet these requirements without substantially driving up costs. Partnerships let governments leverage the investments that other organizations already have made in developing new service lines and delivery channels. For example, sporting goods stores often serve as outlets for fishing licenses, and auto dealerships handle vehicle registrations. Organizations such as the not-for-profit Earth911.org offer community-specific information on all sorts of topics relevant to government —

Types of partnerships

Public-private — Between conventional government procurement and full privatization, many public-private partnership approaches have been developed to serve a wide range of needs. Fully understanding these different types of models, and learning how to use them, can help governments tailor an approach to best meet their particular needs.[49]

Public-nonprofit partnerships can help public agencies fill service gaps, reduce costs, and gain public involvement. When innovations are needed to strengthen the community, public-nonprofit partnerships can achieve better reach, legitimacy, and flexibility than the government acting alone. This category also includes partnerships with institutions of higher learning.

Public-public — Public agencies, even at multiple levels of government, can share information, break down operational silos, and exchange employees to gain particular knowledge and invest jointly to improve performance and outcomes. Partnerships with state universities belong to this category.

from how to legally dispose of used oil and tires, to where to charge electric vehicles.

Customer-facing services, such as renewing drivers' licenses or issuing building permits, are natural candidates for such partnerships. The partnership that created the CityLink private tollway in Melbourne, Australia, introduced a number of customer-friendly innovations to make paying tolls a more positive experience. CityLink delivers alerts to customers' mobile devices when their accounts run low, and it makes house calls to install toll tags on customers' vehicles. An independent body, the CityLink Ombudsman, resolves disputes, and the organization provides transparency and accountability via customer charters and scorecards.

Deploy cutting edge technology

Often, new technology is a key to satisfying citizen demand for better services. But tight fiscal conditions and insufficient staff resources can make it difficult for agencies to deploy the systems they need. Governments can use partnerships to inject innovative technology into their operations, making services both more convenient and efficient.

Oyster card, the contactless "smartcard" launched in 2003 by Transport for London (TfL) in partnership with a private company, allows passengers to "touch in" and "touch out" on the automated barriers. For the customers it has meant cheaper travel without the hassle of standing in queues to buy paper tickets. The card is used to pay for 90 percent of all bus and underground travel in London. After close to three-and-a-half years of operation, TfL decided to upgrade its online system to reduce traffic at ticket offices for payments and top-ups. The existing system was difficult to scale up, expensive, not flexible enough to support promotional offers, and unable to address some quality and security concerns. Partnering with a large private company for online technological innovations, TfL launched a new online system in 2007 that reduced the costs of licensing and hosting by 80 percent, promoted innovative marketing such as offering vouchers for free tracks on iTunes, and provided flexibility to add new applications with no downtime. The private firm is responsible for managing the online system, leaving TfL free to devote its attention to user experience and business processes.[50]

Partnering with private firms with access to state-of-the-art technology can also allow public agencies to solve long-standing problems. Recently, the acceptance of an unsolicited proposal from a private company resulted in the creation of a tunnel to add the missing link to the A86 ring road around Greater Paris, an issue that had remained unresolved for the last 30 years.[51] The tunnel, running under a stretch in West Paris that includes a residential area, historical monuments, and woodlands, will reduce the time of commute between Malmaison and Versailles to 10 minutes, from the 45 minutes it now takes.

Test new approaches

Even the best ideas need to be tested first for their viability. For example, research and past experience of airlines showed that higher toll prices during peak landing times could be used to regulate congestion. However, the feasibility of applying the concept to curb road gridlock needed to be tested. Such road "value pricing" to reduce traffic congestion did not catch on in the United States until the 91 Express Lanes in California ran the first commercial pilot and showed it could work.[52] The model, which gave drivers a choice between using a congested freeway, paying a heftier fee to use a less-congested express lane, or altering their time of travel to avoid super-peak rush hours, has now been replicated across the United States.

Typically, two potential problems prevent public agencies from testing innovative approaches: the risk of spending scarce resources on new projects that may not work; and the lack of metrics to defend these new approaches. Partnerships can help address both challenges.

Gain funds and mitigate risks.

Partnerships can provide the funds needed to create test projects that prove the value of innovative ideas. Just as important, they can help agencies work around bureaucracy that can snuff out new approaches. For instance, when New York City Mayor Michael Bloomberg wanted to transform the city's underperforming public school system, he used partnerships to launch innovative pilot programs and sidestep organizational log jams. One example is the Empowerment Schools program, in which schools sign performance agreements committing them to high levels of student achievement. In return for this commitment, schools receive greater local autonomy over their operations.

Bloomberg used funds from private organizations to test the idea before spending public money on a citywide rollout, a strategy which proved to be key to its success. In the past, school officials might have rejected such a proposal because they deemed it too risky or they could not justify the expense. Recognizing the need to work outside the normal funding process, Bloomberg and Schools Chancellor Joel Klein created the Fund for Public Schools, a nonprofit that attracts private financing for diverse school reforms. The fund allowed Bloomberg to assess and eventually implement innovative programs that otherwise might have been torpedoed by political infighting and budgetary limitations.

In addition, the mayor collaborates with individuals and businesses interested in improving education in New York City. For instance, the city encouraged Joel Greenblatt, a successful hedge fund manager, to create a charter school called the Harlem Success Academy. The academy's business model demands strict accountability and measurable results, and classes are taught by non-union teachers. Greenblatt hopes the program will be replicated across the city. "I'm an investor...I spend my time trying to figure out whether a business model works or not," he said. "I wanted to find a model that worked and roll it out."[53]

Create metrics

The Grameen Foundation, whose goal is to accelerate the process of reducing poverty by increasing the reach of microfinance initiatives, created a Poverty Progress Index that allows microfinance institutions to measure the impact of their program on each client. This is now being used both to report results to donors and other stakeholders and to tailor products to the needs of each client.[54]

Overcome internal constraints

Public agencies face a number of potential barriers to innovation: rigid processes, work force deficiencies, and cultural opposition to deploying new — and sometimes untested — ideas. Partnerships offer a potential way forward. Agencies can leverage the knowledge and abilities of partner organizations to gain crucial new skills. They also can pool resources with partners to extend their reach into desired communities. Ultimately, partnerships can enable public agencies to compensate for weaknesses and improve overall performance.

Use specialized knowledge and skills

Specific knowledge written down in manuals and reports is easy to obtain, but knowledge embodied in individuals does not diffuse as easily.

How can governments use partnering to better tap into such tactic knowledge?

One example is the 4Cs Team formed by the U.S. Department of the Interior to study the barriers in using the new "cooperative conservation" approach to manage natural resources (discussed in chapter 1).[55] The team was populated with employees drawn from the Bureau of Land Management, the Fish and Wildlife Service, and the National Park Service, as well as field managers from the various national parks and refuges. The 4Cs Team looked at barriers and best practices. Members embarked on a series of projects to improve the department's administrative capacity, such as planning, budgeting, and procurement. To make partnering a "way of life at the Department," one of the team's recommendations was to send employees to work in locations that excel at collaboration. Dozens of National Park Service employees, for example, were detailed over time to the Golden Gate National Recreation Area to learn about the park's innovative partnering practices.

Reach deeper into the community

In economically struggling communities, governments often partner with nonprofit organizations to create and diffuse innovations to support the community. In Chicago, the Bethel New Life community-based organization proposed creating the Bethel Center in response to the huge resistance in Chicago's West Garfield Park neighborhood to the transit authority's proposed closure of the elevated Green Line transit rail stop.[56] Bethel used grants from various government agencies and nonprofit foundations to build a three-story, 23,000 square foot, environmentally friendly, state-of-the-art facility across from the transit stop. The facility offered employment counseling and job placement, commercial services, a computer technology center, a 106-child day care center,

and retail space.[57] Not only did the building make it viable for the transit authority to retain the stop in the economically weak neighborhood, the services offered there were decided on by members of the community themselves. The building has become the cornerstone of the community development effort in the area, with 75 new affordable homes built by Bethel in the vicinity of the center. The U.S. Environmental Protection Agency awarded the center its 2006 National Award for Smart Growth Achievement for equitable development.[58]

The Bethel Center is one example of how partnering with the nonprofit sector can help public agencies promote community-centered innovations: the nonprofit developed the infrastructure while the community decided the mix of services that it wanted, making the center more relevant and acceptable.

Overcome resource constraints

Public agencies can often create more value by forming partnerships for collective investments and sharing resources. Pooling resources, including employees and finance, can make it more possible to execute big ideas: the pooled resources help overcome constraints imposed by concerns about risk, tight budgets, and other matters.

Opportunities exist for partnering across multiple levels of government. Summit County, Ohio, and the city of Akron have collaborated on a number of initiatives, including in the Weights and Measures division (to eliminate duplication, all inspection work was shifted to Summit County), law enforcement, and the

Partners produce "God's Own Country"

Kerala, a relatively small state in southern India, identified tourism as a sector it could tap to overcome its economic slump in the early 1990s. But the Kerala Tourism Development Corporation (KTDC), the public sector agency charged with leading the initiative, had accumulated losses of Rs. 89 million, and a number of its hotel projects were running more than a decade late. Further, tourist traffic into the state at the time was insignificant.

In 1992, KTDC formed a joint venture with the Indian Hotel Company (popularly known as the Taj group). The partners structured the deal to bundle together some of the KTDC projects that were losing money and all of its unfinished hotel buildings.[59]

"The JV [joint venture] helped overcome three critical weaknesses of a government organization," says Ashish Kumar Singh, the managing director of KTDC at the time.[60] Public sector agencies have trouble hiring good people. Not only are the salaries low, but the hiring process can take a year or more. The needed talent already existed at the Indian Hotel Company. Second, KTDC did not have the network to market the destination internationally. A private hotel chain had a much greater reach.

Finally, KTDC did not have a brand that would attract investors and customers. Since the law forbade investing outside the state, nobody beyond its borders knew about this organization. Attracting a major hotel chain brought in visibility and attracted a number of other big and small players.[61] All of these developments helped build the brand "Kerala: God's Own Country," which became recognized as a superbrand.

Another significant move was that KTDC leased the properties to the joint venture rather than contributing them as equity. "Kerala pioneered the concept of public-private partnership in tourism in India," says Singh. "All ventures can make losses, particularly in the initial years. This is more so with joint ventures because management practices differ significantly. Financial losses can result in the loss of ownership over properties. We avoided this by instead leasing the properties and contributing equity in cash."

The state government used Rs. 55 million to leverage an investment of Rs. 500 million. Tourist traffic increased by more than 20 percent annually, allowing KTDC to make net profits of Rs. 18.5 million in 1995–96 and 30.1 million in 1996–97.

"Reverse Alert" 911 emergency protocol. The most recent joint effort is the purchase of a single 911 emergency phone system that will display the location of calls made from cell phones on a map at the 911 dispatch center. Purchasing a single system saved the city and county nearly $150,000, and it is expected to lower operating expenses by 40 percent.[62] Summit County and Akron have strengthened their Collaboration Committee to identify new areas for sharing services and resources.

Joint investments by public and private sector organizations also have helped public agencies close skill-set gaps. The joint venture model has been used by several agencies in the United Kingdom. One of the leaders in this trend is British Waterways (BW), which manages more than 2,200 miles of canals in the United Kingdom. The agency formed joint venture partnerships to provide innovative services in a number of areas, including property regeneration, telecommunications, and the operation of waterside pubs. All the earnings from these joint ventures are reinvested by BW into the canal network.

BBC, Britain's government-owned broadcasting company, also formed multiple joint ventures to overcome constraints. The broadcaster struggled with borrowing limits, reduced risk-taking ability, and marketing inexperience that hindered its ability to generate additional revenue. But a 1998 joint venture with the media company Discovery allowed the BBC to greatly expand its reach. The joint venture launched BBC America in the United States and Animal Planet worldwide. In addition, Discovery invested £175 million in factual programs to capitalize on the BBC's reputation.[63]

Benefit from cross-border diffusion

Perhaps one of the biggest benefits of partnering is the pollination of ideas that occurs among participating organizations. As governments outsource or collaborate on a growing number of projects with the private sector, these activities create a growing network of best-practice exchange. Private sector organizations now deliver government services across the globe, giving them the ability to collect and disseminate useful ideas among public agencies worldwide.

For example, Group 4 Falck, a security firm based in Denmark, provides services to governments in more than 80 countries. Organizations of this kind can rapidly diffuse innovation from one jurisdiction to another. This worldwide transfer of innovation is very different from the classical pattern where government officials in different jurisdictions would operate in isolation and make independent decisions about implementing new ideas.

Companies operating in multiple jurisdictions are likely to see connections between rare failures — power blackouts, riots, or attacks on security guards — that could appear as unrelated events to others. This insight helps them manage these crises more successfully. For example, Wackenhut Correction Systems dealt with hunger strikes and protests in its Woomera Detention Center in Australia and its Jamaica Detention Center in New York. Group 4 Falck,

which acquired Wackenhut in 2002, dealt with massive riots in its Yale's Wood Detention Center in the United Kingdom. A corporate provider can harness knowledge gained during one of these crises and apply it effectively to another incident halfway across the world.[64]

Adopt innovations simultaneously

There is also great scope for developing joint solutions to common problems that cut across jurisdictions. An example of this is the Multi-State Clean Diesel Initiative, which required heavy-duty diesel engine manufacturers to abide by strict diesel emission control norms and test procedures in the United States. Simultaneous adoption across states meant not only that the idea diffused faster, but also that state governments avoided falling into a competitive trap by keeping their requirements low.

"There's a way to do it better—find it."

Thomas Edison

Chapter in a box

The partner strategy enables governments to work with other agencies, private industries, universities, and nonprofit organizations to create new solutions. Careful application of the partner strategy allows governments to realize the following benefits:

Seek out new solutions. Partnering offers an opportunity to "buy" innovations from "best-in-class" providers. One of these is state-of-the-art customer service. Citizens have become accustomed to obtaining services from the private sector that cater to certain personal comforts and conveniences. The partnership that created the CityLink private tollway in Melbourne, Australia, offers services, such as installing toll tags, at customers' doorsteps.

Deploy cutting edge technology. Partnering can also enable governments to make use of technology not available in-house. By partnering with a private firm, Transport for London was able to launch a new online system in 2007 that reduced the costs of licensing and hosting by 80 percent, promoted innovative marketing, and provided flexibility to add new applications with no downtime. The private firm is responsible for managing the online system, leaving TfL free to devote its attention to user experience and business processes.

Test new approaches. Even the best ideas need to be tested for viability. Partnering can allow governments to raise funds and mitigate risks for testing new approaches. Mayor Michael Bloomberg used privately funded partnerships with businesses and foundations to test many cutting edge reforms for improving New York's underperforming schools. One example is the Empowerment Schools program, in which schools commit to high levels of student achievement in exchange for greater local autonomy.

Overcome internal constraints. Three initial constraints often block public agencies from improving their performance: lack of flexibility, difficulties in attracting employees with specialized skills, and opposition from multiple stakeholders opposed to new ideas. Partnering strategies can help governments overcome all three.

Use specialized knowledge and skills. The 4Cs Team formed by the U.S. Department of the Interior to study the barriers to using the new "cooperative conservation" approach to manage natural resources was populated with field managers from various national parks and bureaus within the department. To make partnering a "way of life at the Department," one of the team's recommendations was to send employees to work in locations that excel at collaboration.

Reach deeper into the community. The Bethel Center in Chicago, created by the Bethel New Life community-based organization with grants from various government agencies and nonprofit foundations, became the cornerstone of the community development effort in the area.

Surmount resource constraints. Opportunities exist for partnering across multiple levels of government. Summit County, Ohio, and the city of Akron purchased a single 911 emergency phone system that saved nearly $150,000 and is expected to lower operating expenses by 40 percent.

Benefit from cross-border diffusion. Government organizations can also benefit from the diffusion of innovations spawned in other jurisdictions by private sector organizations involved in delivering public services across the globe. Meanwhile, simultaneous adoption of an innovation across multiple jurisdictions can help diffuse ideas that otherwise may not get adopted, such as the Multi-State Clean Diesel Initiative that required heavy-duty diesel engine manufacturers to abide by strict diesel emission control norms.

The partner strategy works best when:
- There is a need to create customer-focused solutions
- The future is uncertain
- The organization needs to benefit from diverse knowledge and the experience of other organizations
- A cross-sector, cross-jurisdiction response is required
- A public sector agency is trying to overcome constraints of scale and cost
- Competition and rivalry between agencies and/or states may restrict change.

5 Network

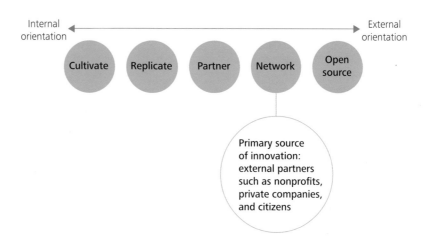

Internal orientation ←——————————————→ External orientation

Cultivate Replicate Partner Network Open source

Primary source of innovation: external partners such as nonprofits, private companies, and citizens

For more than 70 years, the British Broadcasting Corporation (BBC) occupied — and perhaps defined — the cutting edge of content delivery. It pioneered analog broadcasting in 1936, developed stereo for television, and later, made digital audio broadcasting and hi-definition television a reality. As these innovative glory days begin to slip into a bygone era, BBC began to experiment with networks in the hopes of innovating at a faster pace.

For example, Innovation Labs, a series of creative workshops, allows independent media companies to pitch their ideas to the BBC commissioners. The program attracted 29 companies in its first year and generated 170 ideas. Of these, 13 external ideas were selected for further development. The BBC exclusively chooses ideas that can become fully functioning, scaled-up versions (of course, with help from the BBC). The Innovations Labs is now gaining popularity in the United Kingdom, reaching more regions, and building traction among start-up private media companies whose idea-pitching endeavors with a traditional, hierarchical organization like the BBC were, at best, a long shot.

In addition, the BBC is also accessing innovations from its customers. Numerous surveys revealed that the BBC's customers wanted more innovation in their programming and technology choices, so the BBC developed "backstage. bbc.com," a mechanism to invite amateur innovators to use BBC content and tools to build sites and projects that meet the needs of customers in unique and flexible ways. For example, the development community came up with an alternative to seemingly nonsensical, linear newsreels. Rather than relying on headlines like "A1 Cambridgeshire — Narrow lanes both ways at the B1081 Old Great North Road junction in Stamford, speed restriction of 40 kms," the new system combines this linear data with feeds from Google maps that lets readers locate bottlenecks in real time. Similarly, the Homepage Archive came from an independent developer through the backstage initiative.[65] This archive houses all the information published by the BBC and gives users the ability to track the evolution of the homepage and its content from one day to the next.

So while the BBC continues to develop its own internal R&D activities to deliver the next wave of digital technologies, its network strategy ably complements the internal innovation activities. This allows the BBC to tap into its user community as well as source future development ideas from all over the world.

The executives at the BBC will be among the first to tell you that accessing bright ideas from a wide variety of sources can be an effective way to promote and sustain innovation. The network strategy is grounded in the principle that smart people are more abundant than innovative organizations. Good ideas don't have to come from the inside. Sometimes, big challenges call for solutions that are more visible from outside the walls of a given organization.

Governments frequently use the network strategy to deliver services, but they tend to wall themselves in when it comes to innova-tions, despite this strategy's significant benefits in such endeavors. Traditionally, governments have used informal means to garner ideas from outside the public sector, as opposed to a structured, ongoing process. As a result, governments often choose whatever ideas or solutions happen to be popular or most available at the moment a crisis arises.

Networks can be designed to address the most critical challenges facing the public sector's attempts at innovation. The network strategy offers a wide range of benefits (figure 5.1). It gives governments the ability to:

- **Source ideas from anyone.** This releases the pressure on an agency to generate new ideas in a fast-changing world
- **Develop solutions to complex problems.** External individuals and organizations can help develop solutions to complex problems. The role of the agency can shift to identifying worthy solutions to predefined problems
- **Engage citizens and outside groups in policy development and program delivery**
- **Predict which ideas are worth pursuing.** The eyes, ears, and wisdom of citizens can help determine which innovative solutions are worth pursuing
- **Boost responsiveness and create more learning opportunities.**

Figure 5.1: Network strategy of innovation: benefits and approaches

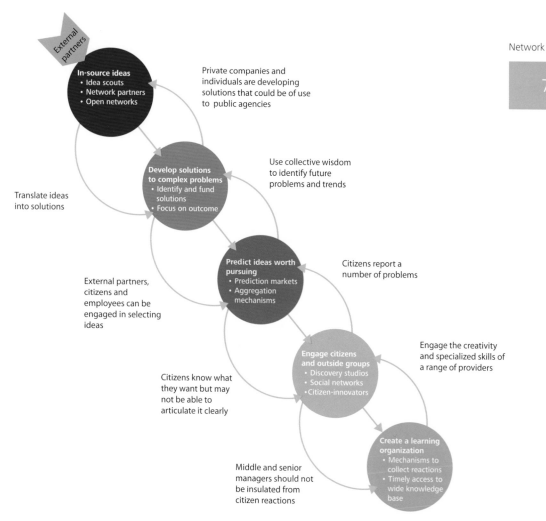

External partners

In-source ideas
• Idea scouts
• Network partners
• Open networks

Private companies and individuals are developing solutions that could be of use to public agencies

Translate ideas into solutions

Develop solutions to complex problems
• Identify and fund solutions
• Focus on outcome

Use collective wisdom to identify future problems and trends

External partners, citizens and employees can be engaged in selecting ideas

Predict ideas worth pursuing
• Prediction markets
• Aggregation mechanisms

Citizens report a number of problems

Engage citizens and outside groups
• Discovery studios
• Social networks
• Citizen-innovators

Engage the creativity and specialized skills of a range of providers

Citizens know what they want but may not be able to articulate it clearly

Create a learning organization
• Mechanisms to collect reactions
• Timely access to wide knowledge base

Middle and senior managers should not be insulated from citizen reactions

In-source innovations and ideas

Many companies are creating sophisticated networks to collect ideas from outside the organization and share skills, knowledge, and physical assets to shape these ideas.[66] For example, the Connect + Develop strategy used by Procter & Gamble (P&G), a leading manufacturer of household and health care products, focuses on establishing networks to leverage the innovation assets of others (figure 5.2).[67] When a "technology entrepreneur" within the company discovered that a Japanese firm was selling melamine foam (traditionally used for soundproofing and insulation) as household sponge, P&G purchased the product from an outside manufacturer and marketed it as Mr. Clean Magic Eraser in the United States and Europe.

Larry Huston, the executive who led the Connect + Develop innovation strategy at P&G, suggests that this model should be considered "in-sourcing" as opposed to "outsourcing." P&G developed an elaborate system of scouts, proprietary networks, external networks, and suppliers to search for adaptable ideas. The new strategy explicitly recognizes that it's a big world out there. Most solutions already exist — somewhere — and most problems are eminently solvable if you ask the right person. This assumption implies that developing an in-house solution from scratch is often unnecessary and expensive. But developing internal capabilities to adapt outside ideas to the needs of P&G's customers is an essential part of the strategy. Implementing Connect + Develop also meant redefining P&G's R&D organization, which encompassed 7,500 people inside the company and about 1.5 million outside.

In the public sector, the Department of Homeland Security (DHS) uses a similar model to solicit ideas from private and public agencies. Using grant money, the Science & Technology Directorate develops formal relationships with academia, think tanks, state and local governments, other public agencies, and private organizations like Google, Apple, and In-Q-Tel to test and prototype emerging technologies.

Develop solutions to complex problems

While tidying his desk, Leon Heppel, a biomolecular researcher at the National Institutes of Health, came across two letters from colleagues. The first, from Earl Sutherland, described the effect of an unusual biomolecule on cells, while the second came from David Lipkin and described the action of a different biomolecule. Heppel soon realized that each of them could benefit from the other's work, so he connected them to each other. This resulted in a series of discoveries and insights that won Sutherland the Nobel Prize in 1971 for discovering the mechanisms of the action of hormones on cells.[68] Organizations such as InnoCentive.com have turned such serendipities in scientific discovery into a science, using a technique called broadcasting.

"Broadcasting" or disclosing an issue to problem solvers outside the research lab can be an effective way to find solutions to difficult scientific problems.[69] A research project de-

Figure 5.2: P&G model for using global networks for innovation

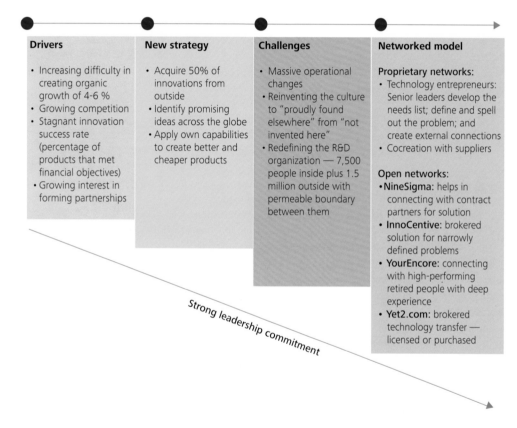

Drivers

- Increasing difficulty in creating organic growth of 4-6 %
- Growing competition
- Stagnant innovation success rate (percentage of products that met financial objectives)
- Growing interest in forming partnerships

New strategy

- Acquire 50% of innovations from outside
- Identify promising ideas across the globe
- Apply own capabilities to create better and cheaper products

Challenges

- Massive operational changes
- Reinventing the culture to "proudly found elsewhere" from "not invented here"
- Redefining the R&D organization — 7,500 people inside plus 1.5 million outside with permeable boundary between them

Networked model

Proprietary networks:
- Technology entrepreneurs: Senior leaders develop the needs list; define and spell out the problem; and create external connections
- Cocreation with suppliers

Open networks:
- **NineSigma:** helps in connecting with contract partners for solution
- **InnoCentive:** brokered solution for narrowly defined problems
- **YourEncore:** connecting with high-performing retired people with deep experience
- **Yet2.com:** brokered technology transfer — licensed or purchased

Strong leadership commitment

signed to measure the efficacy of the broadcasting technique using InnoCentive.com's website showed just this. Of the 166 problems that could not be solved by well-known R&D-intensive firms internally, one third were successfully solved in a limited time (an average of 166 days) by disclosing the problems to outside solvers. Solutions are most likely to come from people either on the periphery or outside the original field of inquiry, using methods that are common in other scientific disciplines. For instance, solutions to one problem —identification of a polymer delivery system — came from an aerospace physicist, a small agribusiness owner, a transdermal drug delivery specialist, and an industrial scientist.

Governments can also adopt this network strategy when faced with big challenges. The CIA, for example, funds a nonprofit organization, In-Q-Tel, to find and deliver technological solutions to the agency for a wide variety of needs, including data mining, strong encryption, and the ability to comb the Web for valuable information. In-Q-Tel provides seed capital to small start-up companies to develop promising new technologies that could generate IT solutions for the CIA. One example is Keyhole, Inc., the company that developed the software now known as Google Earth. Keyhole was founded in 2001, and In-Q-Tel invested in it in February 2003. Google acquired Keyhole in October 2004.[70]

The CIA links to In-Q-Tel through the In-Q-Tel interface center (QIC) located at the CIA's Office of Advanced Information Technology. QIC routes CIA's requirements to In-Q-Tel, which searches through its network for appropriate solutions; QIC then transfers the solutions back to the CIA. QIC also adapts these solutions to the CIA's needs, such as the intelligence agency's stringent security requirements.[71]

Engage citizens and outside groups in policy development and program delivery

As governments grapple with the challenge of creating innovations, the key to gaining input from citizens is to ask the question: What do citizens need? Typically, governments have focused on improving services to citizens in a narrow range of ways: providing easier access to services through the Internet, for instance, or bringing together agencies and levels of government to provide integrated services. Governments need to deliver greater value to citizens in many other areas as well. However, they are not likely to do so unless they develop a deeper understanding of citizen needs.

Focus groups and surveys, though important, do not always do a good job of getting at the unconscious needs of citizens. The interviewer's preconceived notions may limit the questions' effectiveness, since it is hard to ask questions that are out of one's frame of experience. Those being surveyed, in turn, often conform to the "group" or give responses that they think the interviewer wants to hear.

Establish discovery studios

To overcome problems in discovering the deep-seated needs of customers, the consulting firm 4iNNO has created "studio processes" that draw out customer experience on multiple levels. A researcher spends 12 hours with each of five customers over several weeks.[72] The next step is to develop concepts and technologies to solve the problems that emerge from the discussions.

Larry Huston, the former P&G executive who is now managing partner of 4iNNO, explains the studio process: "We have entire protocols that are designed to get at the logic, the emotion, the sensory experience, and the task. It takes 12 hours to do that over multiple weeks with very detailed maps put together. The first consumer will give us 400 concepts, the second consumer will give

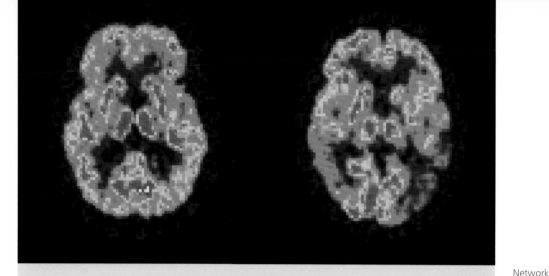

Networked lessons from down under: The Commonwealth Scientific and Industrial Research Organisation (CSIRO), Australia

The networked approach forms the strategic core of the Australian Commonwealth Scientific and Industrial Research Organisation's (CSIRO) efforts to meet major national challenges, create new markets for Australian industry, and fill specific community needs. The government organization brought leading scientific organizations and firms from across the globe into its network and established nine science education centers that attract more than 360,000 students, parents, and teachers annually.

While CSIRO has employed a number of collaborative mechanisms, including formal joint venture arrangements and Cooperative Research Centers, its National Research Flagships Program has been the most effective. In this program, CSIRO recruited 350 partners across industry and research, involving 21 universities.[73] For example, the Australian Imaging Biomarker and Lifestyle (AIBL) Flagship Study targets Alzheimer's disease. The incidence of this leading cause of dementia is rising exponentially in Australia and could affect more than 730,000 people by 2050. To tackle this issue, the Preventative Health National Research Flagship collaborated with the University of Melbourne, Edith Cowan University, Neurosciences Australia, and the Mental Health Research Institute of Victoria to establish the AIBL research cluster. The objective is to develop a holistic solution by involving researchers from a variety of disciplines and connecting cutting edge science with lifestyle and diet studies.

Underpinning the Flagships program is the strategic shift toward a theme-based approach to research that started in 2003. Organizing around themes means focusing on broad issues like climate change, which form the structural backbone of individual research projects. This fosters greater transparency and focus on outcomes. If an individual project runs into problems, resources can be redeployed to another project that accomplishes the theme's goals. The theme-based approach has also improved flexibility in responding to community and industry needs by developing a global network around these themes and adopting a multidisciplinary approach to problem solving. Finally, it has allowed CSIRO to improve risk management by building a portfolio of research streams, ranging from high-risk and long-term projects focused on knowledge building to low-risk and short-term projects that meet very specific industry requirements.[74]

us 400, but there will only be like 200 new, the third will give us 400, and there will be about a 100 new. By the time I get to the fifth consumer, I have elicited the entire experience domain of a targeted group of consumers."[75]

The public sector can tap into two essential needs of citizens, responsiveness and participation, to build trusted relationships and ensure that governments build solutions around citizens' desires, rather than around processes and technology. "Responsiveness" implies that citizens want options to register their views, log complaints, and provide feedback. They want to know that they are being heard and that public officials are actually doing something about what they hear. "Participation" means that citizens want to be involved in creating services and solutions.

Some early movers are taking advantage of this principle to develop citizen-focused solutions. The Australian Taxation Office's "Listening to the Community" program involves its "customers" at every stage in the design process to create a more user-friendly tax system. The office seeks citizen input through multiple methods: field visits, focus groups, prototype development, and product testing. The most important innovation has been the creation of a simulation center where users and designers work together to troubleshoot problems and test products.

Harness social networks

Social networking sites such as YouTube have played a significant role in building brands and promoting companies. The public sector is not completely untouched by this trend, although the best examples emerge from recent political campaigns. In the 2008 U.S. presidential elections, Barack Obama used social networking sites to raise funds, organize volunteers, boost attendance at rallies, and gain the support of young voters.

One of the founders of Facebook, an open source social networking tool, was recruited by the campaign to create MyBo (my.barackobama.com), the campaign's own social networking tool. Supporters could use this tool to organize themselves as they saw fit, without top-down guidance or interference. The network boasts more than 8000 social groups and around half a million members.

The campaign did not focus on providing constant guidance to individual volunteers. Instead, they trained organizers who were then given latitude to innovate locally.[76] These trained and committed supporters then marshaled troops on the ground. They led the door-to-door campaigns. They organized local rallies. They boosted turnout among core supporters. The lesson: online communities can be mobilized to go to work offline.

Elections will never be the same again. The Obama campaign demonstrated that traditional top-down, tarmac-to-tarmac presidential campaigns cannot compete against self-organizing armies of millions motivated by an inspiring candidate and empowered by a Web-savvy campaign team.

It is not only political campaigns, however, that will be transformed by the last election. President Obama's deft use of social networking technologies to create a new campaign model will have big implications for governance. As an example of how governments stand to gain by harnessing social networks, consider the role citizens played in assisting local fire departments during Southern California's wildfires in October 2007 that destroyed nearly 1500 homes and more than 500,000 acres of land.[77] Nearly one million people had to evacuate their homes, dubbed "the largest single peacetime movement of Americans since the Civil War" by NBC Nightly News.[78] It took 19 days to contain the fire. Throughout this period, disaster management and recovery efforts required constant information flow on fire perimeters, evacuation centers, and road closing. Citizens organized themselves rapidly through social networking sites to assist the authorities to coordinate the emergency response: pictures of fires were posted on Flickr; more than 100 social groups sprung up on Facebook to support people affected by the fires; and KNBC.com, a digital news channel, received live streaming video and user-submitted photos.

Government agencies did their bit to harness the collective wisdom. Southern California set up a wiki application where citizens, disaster relief associations, and private companies could get real time information in case of a wildfire breakout in their area. The state's fire agency linked to the Web site of KPBS, a radio station in San Diego, which presented live 24/7 coverage of the wildfires using wikis to coordinate this effort. A fairly new application, My Map, that was earlier used as a fun tool to pinpoint the best places to play golf or get a drink, was reinvented by the employees of KPBS into a virtual map of Southern California with symbols for where to find shelter, what roads were closed, and what had burned. The map attracted more than 1.2 million hits.[79] NASA provided detailed satellite images that showed the active fire zones and the speed at which the fires spread.

Social networking and citizen participation helped meet a number of challenges. Primary among them, the user-generated content helped the coordination of the emergency management effort, thus increasing its efficiency. Citizens remained engaged with the events around them and high levels of awareness helped them respond to rapidly changing events.

In the future, citizens will become more involved in getting the word out about good services and products, and as a result, more people will use them. The role of social networking in "brand building" and processing information is still evolving, and government organizations cannot ignore this trend. Social networking sites are also emerging as a source that companies and government can use to discover customer needs.

Engage citizen-innovators

In the private sector, "lead customers" are increasingly becoming a source of innovation as well as the best predictors of what products and services will find the greatest acceptance.[80] These customers are users who modify existing products to meet their particular needs when the products they need are not available off-the-shelf. The customers' primary purpose in developing these innovations is to benefit from using the improved products rather than profiting from selling them. For example, mountain bikers created tires with armor and metal studs long before manufacturers developed a mountain bike that incorporated these features.

At 3M, lead-user ideas not only outperformed innovations based on traditional market research in generating new product lines (as opposed to spurring incremental change in existing products), they also generated eight times the sales revenue. 3M's lead-user method has two parts. The first step is to identify lead users through person-to-person networks.[81] For example, the 3M team identified lead users of medical imaging through telephone interviews tracing network links and identifying a few radiologists who had created innovations that were more advanced than any commercially available products. These radiologists, in turn, had developed a network with people from other fields who were using a unique approach to solve a similar problem. Military personnel, for instance, were interested in determining whether a particular image was of a rock surface or the tip of an intercontinental ballistic missile. The second step is to transfer knowledge from lead users to the members of the in-house team working on the problem through interviews, site visits, and joint workshops for problem solving. These unique approaches changed both the definition of the problem and the 3M team's final solution.

There are several advantages to engaging lead users in developing innovations. First, users outside an organization who test a variety of ideas vastly outnumber employees engaged in generating innovations. Second, user needs are difficult to identify and transfer to in-house experts, so the entire internal process can be much costlier than allowing users develop their own solutions.

The idea holds true for governments, too. For example, it would be a mistake to assume that governments have to build Web 2.0 applications and social networks from scratch every time. Instead, they could adopt innovative initiatives rolled out by citizens and civil society already engaged in addressing gover-

ing the ingenuity of citizens. Denmark has adopted a user-driven innovation policy to push government organizations and Danish companies to search for innovations among users. A recent program, administered by the Danish Enterprise and Construction Authority (earlier called the National Agency for Enterprise and Construction), budgeted funds (DKK 100 million or around US $17 million a year for four years beginning in 2007) for a number of strategic areas, such as welfare, health, and energy-efficient construction. It also welcomes applications for funding projects outside of these thematic areas as long as they show novelty in user-driven innovation, such as new methods and tools, innovative knowledge dissemination, or competency building.[83]

Predict which ideas are worth pursuing

James Surowiecki's *The Wisdom of Crowds*, explores the delightfully anarchic notion that experts don't come up with the best ideas.[84] Surowiecki's thesis is simple: a large group of people is better at solving a complex problem than an expert, no matter how brilliant. There is a rider, of course: the group should consist of independent, self-interested individuals

nance issues. Consider something like "Fix My Street" in the United Kingdom. It is a Web site built by the voluntary organization My Society to help fix physical problems such as potholes and vandalism in the local community. Users are required to enter their postcode or street name, then click on the exact location on a map of the area, write a detailed description of the problem, and finally add a picture if they would like to. The problem is then sent to the local municipal council. So far, around 25,000 problems have been reported through this site.[82] The site allows more than mere reporting of problems: users can browse problems reported in their area or set up email alerts and RSS feeds to be informed when a problem in their locality gets reported. Governments have the option to simply adopt or partner with such innovative initiatives and thus improve performance at relatively low cost.

Innovative public sector organizations are looking at new ways to create value by leverag-

"Vision without action is merely a dream. Action without vision just passes the time. Vision with action can change the world!"

Joel Arthur Barker

working on a problem in a decentralized way without any direction from the top.

One application of this idea is a "prediction market." Prediction markets (as explained in chapter 1) allow individuals to place "bets" on a final outcome, based on their own personal knowledge. The resultant "odds" are extremely good predictors of the likelihood of the event occurring.

The Pentagon attempted to create a prediction market on economic and political events in the Middle East (dubbed by critics "a futures market in death" or "the terror market"), but an ensuing political uproar over betting on when and where the next terrorist attack or assassination would occur killed the idea. The model continues to gain influence in the private sector, however, and may still have important applications for public sector agencies.

Another option is to use information already available on the Internet, in other media, and in private sources of information. In a recent paper, two Wharton professors showed that wisdom can be downloaded from online crowds. They used the number of documents discussing corruption and other social issues that turn up on an Internet search to rank cities and states for their levels of corruption and other social phenomena that are difficult to measure.[85] This technique could be immensely important to intelligence and law enforcement agencies. Consider the Open Source Center, created by the director of National Intelligence in the United States. It is charged with leveraging open sources of information, such as the news media and commercial databases, to meet the informational needs of a diverse set of clients (foreign coalition partners, local law enforcement agencies, or even the president).

The model has potential application in urban renewal efforts. Cities around the United States already enjoy the inherent efficiencies of the 311 system, but what if a similar mechanism could aggregate already-collected data from this citizen helpline to prevent crises? Such systems already prevent catastrophic impacts on citizens by helping predict areas that will be affected by an incoming storm as well as the problems that will arise.

Boost responsiveness and create more learning opportunities

Networks, when set up correctly, also produce another kind of innovation opportunity. Democratic governance should constantly produce higher-quality services, and citizen reactions to these services are opportunities for innovation. There are a number of ways to collect these reactions: through call centers, on the Web, on the street in conversations between citizens and public servants, in neighborhood centers, and so on. Hierarchical government tends to insulate middle and upper managers from these experiences. In contrast, networked government typically increases the number of individuals working on public service delivery who come in contact with citizens. When supported by good communication and knowledge-management tools, this structure should give government better information about customer

concerns and attitudes, which in turn can boost innovation and responsiveness as well as spread successful practices more quickly.[86]

Networks inherently outperform a single organization when it comes to learning and continuous improvement because they provide timely access to a comparatively broader knowledge base. A neighborhood center that has relationships with multiple providers can more adroitly direct a mother facing abuse, poverty, or other difficulties to the appropriate shelter, counseling, or workforce training than a traditional government agency. A center that is part of a network can engage the creativity and specialized skills of a range of providers while retaining the freedom to adjust its decisions as circumstances change. It can do all that while maintaining its relationship with the mother and her family.

As issues and challenges change, governments must break the barriers and silos that impede the flow of information that becomes knowledge, informed decisions and leads to results. Technology has made it possible for governments to build networks that promote the flow of ideas and information in and out of organizational boundaries. When speed and flexibility are of the essence, all areas of government can benefit from networks to find ideas, inform citizens, and implement solutions.

Chapter in a box

The network strategy utilizes the innovation assets of a diverse base of organizations and individuals to discover, develop, and implement ideas within and outside organizational boundaries. Careful application of the network strategy allows governments to realize the following benefits:

In-source innovations and ideas. Procter & Gamble uses an elaborate system of scouts, suppliers, and open networks such as Yet2.com to identify and adapt promising ideas. This strategy is based on the notion that for every researcher in P&G there are 200 equally competent people outside.

Develop solutions to complex problems. The CIA has funded a nonprofit organization, In-Q-Tel, to find and deliver technological solutions to the agency for its wide variety of needs. In-Q-Tel provides seed capital to small start-up companies to develop promising new technologies that meet the CIA's needs.

Engage citizens and outside groups in policy development and program delivery. Delivering greater value to citizens requires a deeper understanding of citizen needs. There are several ways governments can do this:

Establish discovery studios. This is a mechanism to discover the deep-seated, often unconscious needs of customers by mapping their entire experience domain.

Harness social networks. Citizens can be engaged to get the word out about government services and programs through social networks.

Engage citizen-innovators. Citizens can become an important source of ideas and help to identify future trends, reduce costs, and test a variety of ideas that may not otherwise be possible. An example of this is the BBC backstage initiative that allows users to submit a variety of prototypes.

Predict which ideas are worth pursuing. Prediction markets can aggregate the knowledge of a large number of people to predict future events. The principle, however, extends beyond prediction markets. For example, water-logging complaints at the 311 service predict problems that arise during a storm, pinpoint the affected areas, and prevent catastrophic impact on citizens.

Boost responsiveness by creating more learning opportunities. Networked government typically increases the number of individuals working on governmental matters who come in contact with citizens. Networks also provide more timely access to a broader knowledge base than is possible within a single organization.

The network strategy works best when the government needs to:
- Find the "best" solution to a problem
- Keep ideas flowing in
- Aggregate information across a diverse group of people
- Use the information available from users to select the best solution to a problem
- Tap into myriad perspectives
- Understand conscious and unconscious needs of consumers
- Get users to design solutions that best meet their needs
- Create multiple access points to customers
- Take advantage of dispersed knowledge.

6 Open source

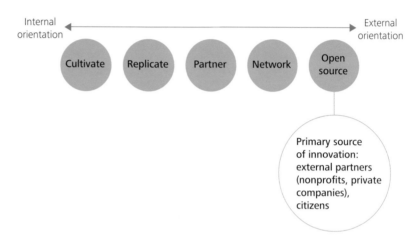

As the network strategy found greater acceptance in the private sector, the software community embraced an even more radical model: open source innovation. This model stretches the idea of networking to its extreme form: anyone and everyone are invited to contribute ideas and innovations with limited managerial supervision.

One public sector example is World Wind, a software program developed by the National Aeronautics and Space Administration (NASA) that lets people zoom in on virtually any place on earth and view it in a video-game-like three-dimensional format using satellite imagery. It was released as a freely available open source program in August 2004. The open source model offered NASA the opportunity to build specialized functionalities by outsourcing the development work to the world community. Around 100,000 users downloaded the program in the first week. With the use of a wiki to suggest code modifications, the software program has evolved continuously, adding new data and 3D imagery of the Earth and Moon, and images of other planets, stars, and galaxies. Users have set up a web site that provides instructions on how to use the World Wind program as well as developed add-on applications that make it easier to find specific locations such as the Apollo landing sites.[87]

World Wind has found varied and unexpected applications. The U.S. Naval Research Laboratory, located in California, provides real time weather information via World Wind by integrating weather imagery with high-resolution data sources. NASA has also signed agreements with Australia and the United Kingdom to develop tenth grade curriculum on the "origins of life" using World Wind and other tools.

The World Wind program came out of a skunk works project at NASA Learning Technologies (NLT), which incubates innovative technologies to deliver educational content into the classroom. Releasing World Wind as an open source program helped further NLT's mission by offering a platform for others to build on by adding information and intelligence. It also helped improve the software quality through peer review, and increased dissemination and awareness.

The open source software movement, as the World Wind example shows, harnesses the knowledge of countless unrelated individuals to build and maintain complex, world-class systems. Open source models, such as the Linux operating system, the Firefox Web browser, and the Wikipedia online encyclopedia seek solutions to clearly defined problems from enthusiasts, irrespective of their specialization. They are freely available; individuals improve them out of a sense of community or a desire to create something new.

The open source movement has several distinct features:

- Countless unrelated individuals voluntarily come together to create complex, world-class systems
- Ownership does not reside with an individual or an organization

- Everyone can contribute ideas and help develop the product
- Users decide how they want to utilize innovative end products, which leads to new applications.

The open source innovation strategy has largely been ignored outside the software community. Most people treat it as a special case. Open source, however, is an archetype that can be applied successfully to endeavors well outside the realm of software, though likely to be facilitated by technology tools. However, to some people the strategy sounds too good to be true — why would people participate in an initiative when there are no financial rewards or guaranteed outcomes?[88] Apart from an enhanced reputation and the value one derives from using the product, participating in open source communities captures the imagination of those involved and challenges contributors to be creative, learn from the experience, and enjoy the task. This is what the public sector can benefit from.

An open source innovation strategy, when structured well, can produce the following critical benefits for the public sector (figure 6.1):

- **Create repositories of ideas and tools.** The real benefit of the open source strategy is that users do not need to wait for upgrades and enhancements
- **Build in mechanisms for continuous improvement.** The broader community can discover where problems exist and make the required fixes
- **Gain customized solutions at**

96

Figure 6.1: Benefits of the open source innovation model

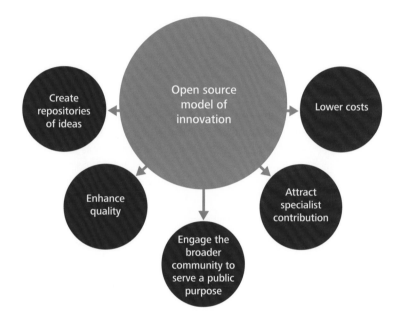

minimal cost. Dealing with uncertain fiscal realities requires governments to find low-cost solutions without compromising performance and responsiveness. Open source enables governments to gain customized solutions with minimal investment

- **Attract specialist contributions.** The open source strategy allows governments to tap into specialized expertise from outside the organization

- **Engage the broader community to serve a public purpose.** Governments can engage citizens

in increasing social welfare by supporting their ability to innovate.

Build repositories of ideas and tools

Governments across the world are facing several challenges that require innovative responses. For instance, one of the downsides of globalization has been the loss of manufacturing and service jobs in advanced economies. To maintain competitiveness, advanced economies will need to press forward with reforms in education, especially in teaching math and science to high school students.

Officials with the government of Ontario, Canada, realized that they had to do something creative to provide a flexible educational plan customized to the learning choices of teenagers to help them develop solid reading, writing, and math skills. The province also needed to develop resources for small schools and isolated students. Ontario's targets include "75 percent of students achieving at the provincial standard in literacy and numeracy by 2008 and 85 percent of students graduating from high school by 2010–11."[89]

To meet these objectives, Ontario has employed the open source strategy with its E-Learning Ontario initiative. It built an online repository of resources developed by teachers that can be customized to local needs and made this cache of information available to teachers and students at no cost. Credit courses, a technical help desk, and professional development programs for teachers and school board members are available free of charge. This repository is especially useful to small, rural, and isolated schools that face shortages of educational resources and specialized teaching staff.

The E-learning initiative signifies the most important aspects of the open source strategy. To begin with, open source strategy is not a limited applications paradigm. Its principles are likely to find use outside the software community. Further, open source is not merely about creating and accessing free products; it is a completely different way of organizing and functioning.

Build in mechanisms for continuous improvement

Open source projects such as E-learning Ontario are particularly useful in reducing complexity and enhancing quality. Due to the remoteness of the participants and the decentralized nature of development, the solutions tend to be modular and well documented. This means that complex projects are broken down into manageable tasks performed by various groups based on their unique skills and interest. Detailed information is made available on every aspect of the solution development to make it easier for people not involved in the development of the module to comprehend, synchronize, and further develop the content.

Quality is further enhanced as a diverse group of users can fix problems on the fly. The more widely available the programs or source code are for public testing and experimentation, the more rapidly problems can be fixed and improvements made. As Eric Raymond writes: "Given enough eyeballs, all bugs are shallow," meaning that as long as you have enough users looking for the bugs in the code they will be found.[90] This, for instance, was the primary reason NASA released World Wind as an open source program.

These open source principles are now being applied to create strategic visions and policy documents. The city of Melbourne in the state of Victoria, Australia, used the wiki technology to place the city plan online as a shared document to be edited by the public. The Future Melbourne plan document will create a shared vision for 2020 and beyond.

The consultation process, which lasted from May 17 to June 14, 2008, offered all the benefits of the open source strategy. For instance, citizens could adopt a modular approach, dividing work into fixing typos, reformatting, reorganization of content, and ideation. A large number of participants, some 6500, contributed based on their skills, interests, and competencies to enhance the quality of the document.

Future Melbourne extended the notion of participatory governance way beyond anything achieved so far, whether through town hall meetings or focus groups to consult citizens. The use of discussion pages, one for each page on the plan document, allowed iterative and integrated development of the plan with participants evaluating and addressing changes and comments. It meant that carefully thought-out edits to the plan, when well defended with comments on the discussion page, were less likely to be modified. Participation could take numerous forms: citizens making direct changes on the plan document, seeking a response from an officer, or refining an idea. Others could choose to merely inform themselves and build awareness.

Gain customized solutions with minimal investment

The District of Columbia launched a contest called Apps for Democracy that invites open source Web applications to convert real time data from multiple government agencies into an accessible and usable format. Open source was not an option; all submissions had to be released in open source code. For an investment of $50,000, the District of Columbia government received 47 applications, worth an estimated $2.7 million in benefits, in 30 days.

The top prize was awarded to iLive.at. Through this application, all citizens need to do is enter their address and iLive.at provides them with neatly organized information tailored to their location. To know where the nearest shopping center or post office is, look under the "errands" category. Click on "crimes" and you get all the recently reported offenses in your area. Demographic information is available in the "people" category. These innovative applications are expected to help government organizations improve performance and increase responsiveness to citizens.

Governments collect an immense amount of data that remain largely unanalyzed. It is possible to convert this data into information with very little investment. In the words of Vivek Kundra, chief technology officer of the District of Columbia Government: "There is immense creativity out there and you can do it for very little money by democratizing data."[91] In difficult economic times, the open source strategy is a powerful mechanism for stretching scarce dollars further.

Initiatives like Apps for Democracy will likely become harbingers of a new age of participatory governance. "We need to think of citizens as people who can co-create," continues Kundra. "The idea was to get the best thinking using data feeds to develop applications. My goal is to put as much data out there as possible."[92]

Open source diffusion lessons from Wikipedia

Wikipedia offers an interesting example of how diffusion is ingrained in the open source strategy. Wikipedia is an online encyclopedia where all content can be read, edited, copied, and even sold as long as the authorship rights are passed on to people receiving the content. In short, all users of the content on Wikipedia must confer freedom to use and reuse the content on everyone who comes across that content.

One of the guiding principles of the open source strategy is the democratic process. This again is visible in the way Wikipedia functions: decisions are not imposed from the top but come from the bottom up. When people contribute content to Wikipedia, there is no guarantee that it will appear unchanged. The content is verified to the extent possible by the wider community and edited to ensure that it meets its requirements of verifiability, language, and neutrality. Any content that is not based on verifiable sources is marked for editing or deletion. At times, disputes result in "edit wars" or feverish editing of content by separate groups in an attempt to ensure that their point of view is accepted as the final one. Edit wars go against the established policy of consensus building and are strongly discouraged.

Edit wars and other conflicts are initially handled through the democratic process. For instance, users may ask for a third opinion on the topic or request informal mediation.

However, there are limits to the extent of democracy in an open source model. A look at Wikipedia's dispute resolution process makes this point clear.[93] Registered users can edit content, move pages, or start new articles. Above the registered users are those who have permission to roll back a page to its previous version if there is an unacceptable change. Administrators, who number around 1,500 and are selected by the Wikipedia community through an established process, have the right to delete pages, freeze content on a page to be edited only by other administrators, and block delinquent users from editing a page. Above the administrators are bureaucrats who have higher privileges including the liberty to promote people to the level of administrator. Finally, there is an arbitration committee of about a dozen users that acts as the final touch point for dispute resolution. Any decision made by the arbitration committee is binding on all parties.

In very rare cases, the Wikipedia Board of Trustees, the ultimate corporate authority for the Wikipedia Foundation, Inc., can step in to resolve a dispute. In open source strategy, the project organizer or the "core" is responsible for ensuring that all possible solutions are in line with its objectives. In the case of disputes, the core becomes the final arbiter and the ultimate decision rests with it.

There are three elements of diffusion that government agencies can abstract from the Wikipedia example. First, diffusion is about sharing ideas and building on them. The freedom to use and reuse Wikipedia content ensures that individuals benefiting from an innovation cannot prevent others from benefiting from their improvements to it. Second, diffusion is about gaining buy-in from all stakeholders. This requires elaborate arrangements to handle disputes without interfering with the creative process. Finally, there have to be both informal and formal mechanisms to deal with disputes. This means that managerial attention can be focused on disputes that require the most attention; the low-scale disputes will work themselves out.

Attract specialist contributions

A peer reviewed pilot called the Peer-to-Patent Project in the U.S. Patent and Trademark Office employs the open source model. Software patents are particularly difficult to grant because of issues around databases, protocols, and date stamps. Publications and references can raise questions about the originality of a patent application. Dates associated with this "prior art" go a long way in deciding whether or not to grant a patent. Litigation history suggests that patent examiners make the best choice when prior art is included in the application. It was thought that opening the process of identifying prior art and permitting everyone (especially software professionals) to submit prior art could help patent examiners make faster and better decisions.

However, the Peer-to-Patent project needed to ask whether people have enough motivation to participate in the program. The project offers no monetary incentive and the patent ensures exclusive rights rather than common ownership of new products.[94] Another issue concerns whether patent applicants will agree with, and use, this model. Intellectual property that goes out to the public may defeat the purpose of filing a patent in the first place. The motivating factors that usually spur people to participate in open source efforts may restrict involvement.

So far these challenges have proven quite manageable. The project was launched June 15, 2007, and as of January 2009, 2416 people had signed up to be reviewers and cited 301 instances of prior art on 50 applications.[95]

Open source organizers have several options for attracting people to their projects.

For example, the Peer-to-Patent project cites the names of those who have submitted prior art with their profile and photograph, the type of submission, and reference to the patent application to which the prior art is applicable. Others offer cash rewards, or in some extraordinary cases, employment to those who help make the final decisions.

Engage the broader community to serve a public purpose

Governments are beginning to realize the power of the largely self-sustaining open source movement to shape a knowledge society that meets the needs of citizens. One example is the European Commission's effort to promote "science shops." In the early 1970s, a group of Dutch students got together to solve scientific problems for their nonprofit clients. They created links between academia and civil society to solve problems, such as soil pollution, that affect daily life. This effort produced the first "science shop," sparking a movement that spread across countries, creating a global network of shops that shared knowledge and expertise. The movement grew through volunteers and students. To encourage students to join these groups, many universities today offer academic credit for their participation. The European Commission funds science shop projects benefitting local civil society organizations without the means to conduct such research. Further, it promotes activities that encourage networking among science shops to help spread the movement across the European Union.

Typically, the science shops work with community groups facing a pressing problem. Financial reimbursement of the project cost may be a part of this deal, but it usually does not cover the salaries of researchers and administrative staff. The projects and issues addressed by science shops range from pure sciences and engineering issues to studies involving psychological, social, and legal analysis. Examples include a study on the reasons for social exclusion of elderly men in Belfast, United Kingdom, and the development of a computer game for children with speech disorders in Lynby, Denmark.

"By supporting citizens in their quest for knowledge, people are given more possibilities to take responsibility for shaping their own life and their living environment," says Maria van der Hoeven, Dutch minister of Education, Culture, and Science. In Canada, the Social Sciences and Humanities Research Council is one of two government-backed agencies channeling funds to research projects jointly undertaken by universities and community organizations.[96]

Some people believe that the open source movement cannot sustain itself in the private sector merely on the basis of altruism or enthusiasm. Larry McVoy, one of the early supporters of the open source software movement, believes that the model is not a viable way to produce products and services: "The bottom line is you have to build a financially sound company with a well-trained staff. And those staffers like their salaries. If everything is free, how can I make enough money to keep building that product for you and supporting you?"[97] This is where governments might step in. If companies cannot support open source efforts that benefit society at large because these projects

do not provide a revenue stream, the government could consider helping to fund them.

How to build an open source initiative

An open source model operates at three levels (figure 6.2). At the core is the project creator who defines the goals and objectives and also functions as the final mediator for dispute settlement. The "development community" surrounds this core. The function of this community is to build solutions, communicate with peers, send its feedback to the core, and when required, be the mediator between the core and the users. The last layer is the user community. This community accesses the products and services, customizes them, and is intricately involved in the development process.

Building and sustaining an open source initiative has five main components:

1. Develop an infrastructure that supports the open source model
2. Build a community of collaborators
3. Promote flexibility and open knowledge sharing
4. Democratize the innovation process
5. Create feedback loops.

Develop an infrastructure that supports the open source model

The National Aeronautics and Space Administration (NASA) launched a small open source project called "ClickWorkers," which uses public volunteers to identify and catalog craters on the surface of Mars from a freely

Figure 6.2: The open source innovation model

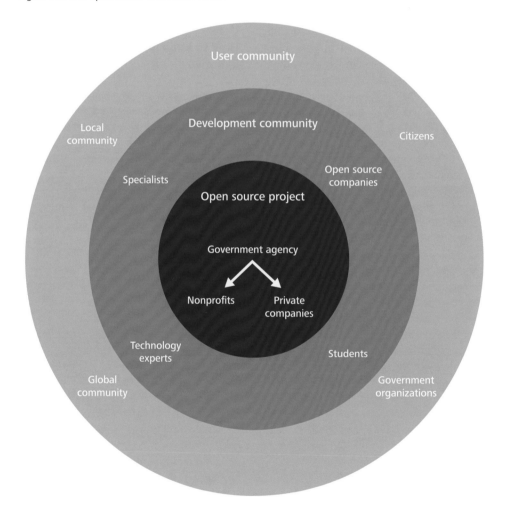

available satellite image. NASA created a Web site and a database and left the "clickworkers" to decide where and for how long they chose to work. The work does not require a lot of scientific training, so NASA can benefit from wide participation. Normally, this kind of effort would entail months of work by scientists, but it requires only one engineer, working part-time, to maintain the Web site.

There are a few questions that project organizers need to ask themselves to create an open database. What kind of information do developers need to create a solution? How will they input their response? How will they record these responses? How can they avoid duplication of data and responses? How will they validate the data?

The principle behind open source strategy is to provide all the information to users so they can use resources as they see fit. In the software sector, this means giving access to the source code, which gives users the ability to customize it, facilitate cross-organization application sharing, and realize cost savings through reduced licensing and hosting fees. The distribution model also involves free access to anyone who wants to use the content. For example, the MIT OpenCourseWare initiative provides open access to lecture notes, related collaterals, and exams to anyone who wants to see it. In November 2007, Verizon Wireless opened its network to mobile devices to stimulate innovations from developers and provide greater flexibility to customers in using software. The more these developers identify and meet customer needs, the stronger the Verizon network becomes relative to other networks.

Questions that can help decide the best form of distribution mechanism include: Who will benefit from the innovation? How would the target group prefer to access your products? What channels for distribution are available to you? How can you reduce the effort required in accessing the open source material?

Build a community of innovators.

Before citizens can be engaged to contribute to an open source project, government agencies need to get the ball rolling. This can be tricky. The Internet is full of open source projects that remain ignored by the wider community. Do you build the infrastructure and then wait for others to join the bandwagon? How do you ensure that the money spent on an open source project is not wasted? The dilemma is well expressed by Beth Noveck, the New York Law School professor credited for bringing the peer review process to patent examination: "My greatest fear was being the kid who gives a birthday party and no one comes."[98]

Building a community that has deep interest in the subject is important. The Future Melbourne project had a yearlong phase of collecting citizen submissions online and discussion forums organized by the Future Melbourne team that helped raise awareness and interest. Only after this phase was complete was the draft placed online for editing. The project also had a reference group of prominent leaders and thinkers from the public, private, and nonprofit sectors. They not only provided guidance and support but also worked as champions for the initiative.

A community of open source collaborators can also be created through contests that give out cash prizes as the District of Columbia did with its Apps for Democracy initiative. The real benefit for the open source community, however, may lie beyond the financial gains; winning a contest can be an end in itself, irrespective of the prize money.

As the Apps for Democracy and Future Melbourne initiatives have shown, network effects are important in building open source communities.

Promote flexibility and open knowledge sharing

Open source development gives governments the ability to reduce costs by building systems and solutions that can be reused by others. For example, now that Ontario has already created the E-Learning online repository, it should be possible for other governments to take a large part of the content and modify it for the purposes of their own constituents. In other words, there is no need for governments to spend taxpayer money in duplicative efforts when much of the functionality of a system is common across agencies, regions, and levels of government.

This flexibility will not occur, however, unless governments share their resources in a systematic way. This requires careful consideration of an innovation's relevance in new contexts. How can governments create something using preexisting modules or self-contained elements of a new initiative? How can third parties help customize the innovation?

Most individual efforts to develop a vaccine for AIDS over the last two decades have been disappointing, with long delays in publishing results and competing or redundant work being carried out by rival research teams. Microsoft founder and philanthropist Bill Gates believes that a completely new approach is required to get results faster. The Bill and Melinda Gates Foundation funds only those AIDS vaccine researchers who agree to share their results with others. It is expected that the open sharing of data and information will allow researchers to build on past successes and failures and increase the pace of discovery.

Democratize the innovation process

In an open source model, no single individual or organization calls the shots. DemocracyLab, a nonprofit organization, aims to create an online forum for "producing collaborative solutions to public policy problems." Participants can contribute their opinions online, as well as express their level of agreement with opinions expressed by others. The motivation is to develop solutions using the principles of direct democracy. The best possible opinions would likely get a higher number of votes and rise through the noise of all the potential public policy positions. Among other benefits, this would help governments understand citizen needs, allow elected officials to test possible alternatives, and build consensus on important issues.

The open source culture is about building on past successes and not repeating mistakes. This is the guiding motive of open source strategy

rather than an offshoot of the process. Not repeating others' mistakes is possible only when data, resources, and knowledge are shared openly in a democratic environment. To be successful, the open source culture requires a shift in mindset away from secrecy and suspicion.

Create feedback loops

As mentioned earlier, one of the important roles of the "development community" is to provide continuous feedback. Feedback mechanisms can take a variety of forms. Based on its interactions with the user group, the development community provides detailed documentation of successes and failures and what needs to change. It tests options on a limited scale to see whether changing some parts would make the overall program more effective. Tools such as wikis and blogs are used to create community groups to discuss options and share experiences. Constant feedback is critical for promoting continuous innovation and flexibility.

The examples cited here offer only a small window into the possibilities for improving governance and service delivery by tapping into open source models. The open source strategy has been fruitfully employed by governments to tackle challenges in education, technology, and patenting. The greatest limit to the application of this concept will be our finite imaginations.

Chapter in a box

The open source innovation strategy entails a shift away from knowledge "monopolies" to an open source model that encourage many people to collaborate voluntarily to develop ideas and create solutions. This strategy can allow governments to achieve the following benefits:

Benefits of the open source innovation model

Build repositories of innovative ideas and tools. Officials with the government of Ontario, Canada, realized that they had to do something creative to provide a flexible educational plan that is customized to the learning choices of teenagers to help them develop solid reading, writing, and math skills. To meet these objectives, they built an online repository of resources developed by teachers that is available to teachers and students at no cost and can be customized to local needs.

Enhance quality by creating mechanisms for continuous improvement. The more widely available programs are for public testing and experimentation, the more rapidly problems can be fixed and improvements made. This was the primary reason NASA released World Wind as an open source program. The city of Melbourne in the state of Victoria, Australia, used wiki technology to place the city plan online as a shared document to be edited by the public.

Gain customized solutions with minimal investment. The District of Columbia launched a contest called Apps for Democracy that invites open source Web applications to convert real time data from multiple government agencies into an accessible and useable format. For an investment of $50,000, the District of Columbia government received 47 applications in 30 days, worth around $2.7 million in benefits.

Attract specialist contributions. A U.S. Patent & Trademark Office peer reviewed pilot called the Peer-to-Patent Project permits anyone to submit prior art that could help patent examiners make faster and better decisions. As of January 2009, 2416 people had signed up to be reviewers and had cited 301 instances of prior art on 50 applications

Engage the broader community to serve the public. Using an open source model, government can attract innovative people to important projects and connect diverse organizations and individuals in a manner where they augment each other's capacity to produce an important public outcome. Governments could also consider funding open source initiatives that are not self-financing because they do not provide a consistent revenue stream but are doing work that benefits society at large.

Building an open source initiative

An open source initiative requires creating a physical infrastructure that supports the activities of the open source community, building a community of collaborators, and at a more abstract level, creating mechanisms for sharing knowledge and information in a democratic environment.

Create open database and distribution mechanisms. NASA has created a Web site and a database to allow public volunteers to identify and catalog craters on the surface of Mars from a freely available satellite image. The "clickworkers" decide where and for how long they choose to work.

Build a community. Future Melbourne project had a yearlong phase of collecting citizen submissions online and discussion forums organized by the Future Melbourne team that helped raise awareness and interest. The project also had a reference group of prominent leaders and thinkers who provided guidance and support, and worked as champions for the initiative.

Promote flexibility and open knowledge sharing. There is no need for governments to spend taxpayer money in duplicative efforts when much of the functionality of a system is common across agencies, regions, and levels of government. This flexibility will not occur, however, unless governments share their resources in a systematic way.

Democratize the innovation process. DemocracyLab, a nonprofit organization, allows participants to contribute their opinions on public policy problems online, as well as express their level of agreement with opinions expressed by others. Among other benefits, this would help governments understand citizen needs, allow elected officials to test possible alternatives, and build consensus on important issues.

Create feedback loops. Constant feedback is critical for promoting continuous innovation and flexibility. In an open source project, the development community documents successes and failures and provides feedback to the "core" on what needs to change. It also tests options on a limited scale to see whether changing some parts would make the overall program more effective.

The open source strategy works best when:
- You are engaging people from diverse disciplines
- You need large-scale collaboration
- Accomplishing a task within a single organization would require more time and resources than it can provide
- Knowledge is tacit and resides in people rather than manuals, research papers, articles, or others
- The benefits are widely dispersed
- Users need flexibility in usage and can customize the solution to their needs
- Protecting intellectual property is not a very large concern.

Part 3:
The innovation organization

7 Sustaining a culture of innovation

Many public sector organizations make sporadic efforts to encourage innovation, but few implement the formal changes needed to spark transformational change. Without altering traditional roles, processes, and organizational structures, innovation initiatives become mired in bureaucracy and fail to deliver fundamental change.

The innovation strategies discussed in chapters 2–6 evolved as ways to overcome the barriers to innovation created by unwieldy bureaucratic structures in large organizations. Over the long term, however, organizations married to rigid standard procedures are unlikely to bring about lasting change, irrespective of which strategy is adopted. Nor will the ability of an organization to manage an innovation cycle improve. Some changes in organizational structures are typically necessary to make optimal use of innovation strategies.

The organizational model in the public sector has changed little over the last century. Spawned by the factories in the nineteenth century that wanted "hands and legs," employees mostly operated in a rule-based, hierarchical system. The public sector tended to invent most things in-house. A typical response to a problem was to throw resources and experts at it and hope for the best result.

The 1980s saw a growing emphasis on partnerships. These required public sector managers to acquire new skills and think beyond the notion of "government knows best." However, public agencies changed little in their internal organization, and most people continued to regard government as the primary owner and provider of public services.

Emerging organizational models, such as the networked approach discussed in chapter 5, require a bigger and more fundamental change. Public sector organizations may no longer always own the services they provide. Instead, they are often aggregators and managers of services provided by others. This new model requires governments to gather ideas from anywhere and tap talent markets far and wide. Agencies then use internal skills to adapt these ideas to their specific needs.

The strategies for innovation outlined in previous chapters will challenge public sector organizations to rethink their boundaries, and create new, more flexible, structures (figure 7.1).

Figure 7.1: The evolving organizational structure of government agencies

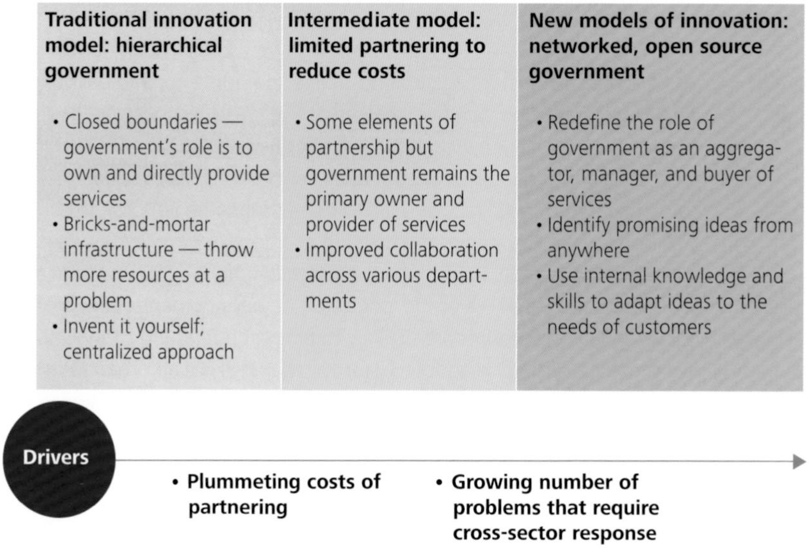

Traditional innovation model: hierarchical government	Intermediate model: limited partnering to reduce costs	New models of innovation: networked, open source government
• Closed boundaries — government's role is to own and directly provide services • Bricks-and-mortar infrastructure — throw more resources at a problem • Invent it yourself; centralized approach	• Some elements of partnership but government remains the primary owner and provider of services • Improved collaboration across various departments	• Redefine the role of government as an aggregator, manager, and buyer of services • Identify promising ideas from anywhere • Use internal knowledge and skills to adapt ideas to the needs of customers

Drivers →

• **Plummeting costs of partnering**

• **Growing number of problems that require cross-sector response**

Redefine organizational boundaries

In today's world, no single organization, private or public, will likely have the ability to develop all necessary innovations in-house. Neither can they afford to ignore internal capabilities. What organizational structures best enable the innovation approaches outlined previously in the book? The answer may lie in the specific needs and capabilities of a given organization: the greater the need to search for ideas and innovations from outside, the more useful is a networked organizational model.

Procter & Gamble (P&G), discussed in

chapter 5, developed a networked model called Connect + Develop to tap into talent residing outside its organizational boundaries (figure 7.2). P&G's network strategy encompasses everything from creating mechanisms to ensure day-to-day accountability to developing new programs and a new vision. The company encourages ideas to flow from external sources as well as from its own employees.

Australia's Commonwealth Scientific and Industrial Research Organisation (CSIRO) also adopted a networked organizational model to help drive innovation. Rapid globalization in the 1990s spurred demand for globally relevant

Figure 7.2: Network organization model: the case of Procter & Gamble

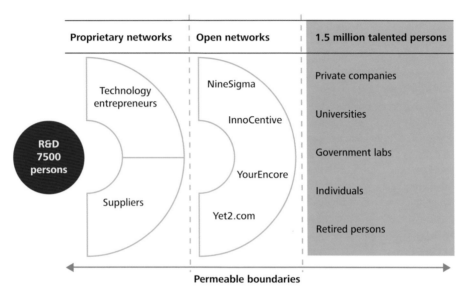

knowledge. CSIRO, a heavily siloed and internally focused organization, needed a window to the outside world — both for bringing in new ideas and disseminating them. Further, the organization was under growing pressure to justify its investments and deliver results. To address these requirements, CSIRO launched its Flagship program, which created research partnerships with industry, government, and other research bodies. These partnerships are organized around large scale themes, such as energy, light metals, and water.

To support the new approach, CSIRO transformed its organizational structure by aligning divisions around desired outputs and then giving control over those outputs to the individual divisions. This initiative had four critical elements: shift the focus from input to output, centralize all support services, adopt a matrix organizational structure, and implement a new software solution. These elements were meant to act like glue, holding the networks of the organization together in a web-like structure.

Catherine Livingstone, who chaired the CSIRO board for five years during the transformation, said the changes were necessary in an era of global competition. "CSIRO comprised many disparate divisions working within — but not for — CSIRO," she said. "This was not sustainable at a time of mounting pressure on CSIRO to demonstrate what the government was getting for its investment — especially given that CSIRO was no longer the only major research centre available."[99]

It was increasingly difficult for CSIRO to justify its existence purely on the basis of national interest. Stakeholders wanted justification in terms of numbers, results, and financial sustainability. CSIRO also realized that industry would not accept research with long lead times and uncertain results, particularly when the same research could be done faster and cheaper elsewhere in the world.

The Flagship program created global partnerships in key areas of interest to industry and government. These activities were designed to help develop new markets and provide a competitive edge to Australian industry. The networked model let CSIRO forge deeper ties with business and industry around each of the thematic areas, allowing it to market ideas faster and better commercialize its research.

Although both P&G and CSIRO adopted the networked model in order to create new windows into the outside world, neither organization ignored its internal capabilities. Instead, internal staff developed new talents. For example, P&G created a network of technology entrepreneurs who fostered relationships with universities, industry researchers and suppliers, and defined problems for them to solve. P&G also developed mechanisms to neutralize internal resistance from employees

who feared the new strategy would diminish P&G's internal capabilities or cut jobs. Reward programs were established that recognized employee contributions regardless of where ideas originated. Further, P&G employees were offered training to acquire new skills in evaluating, screening, and developing ideas, including during risky scale-ups.

Traditional innovation strategies such as cultivation, and newer models such as open source and networking, can coexist in organizations seeking to redefine their boundaries. As discussed in chapter 2, safe havens such as skunk works are the key to solving some of the toughest challenges that require systemic innovations and involve core activities that require tapping into the wisdom of employees. Skunk works also offer a potential mechanism to evaluate, screen, and develop ideas flowing in from outside. Organizations looking to shift to new models of innovations should take care not to compromise internal capabilities.

While redefining the organizational boundary is critical to successful adoption of the networked and open source models of innovation, its purpose can vary based on the unique needs of the organization. The P&G model is particularly focused on strengthening the idea generation process. The CSIRO model extends the notion of networking to implementing ideas. Redefining organizational boundaries, therefore, need not be seen as a generic principle. Rather, based on its strengths and weaknesses, each organization needs to carefully match strategies with stages in the innovation process.

Figure 7.3 Innovation strategy of the technology strategy board

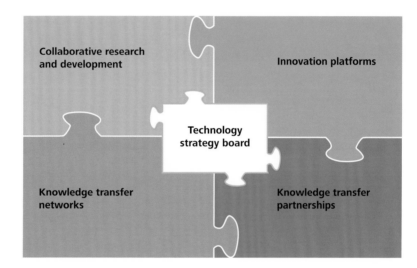

Take an integrated view

The Technology Strategy Board in the United Kingdom, an example of a skunk works in the public sector, uses multiple strategies to translate knowledge residing in various organizations into innovations (figure 7.3). It identifies key technology areas, such as nanotechnology, bioscience, and information and communication technology, that are strategically important to the United Kingdom and that can help the government create or sustain leadership in emerging products, services, and processes. The board sets priorities in consultation with members of the private sector and uses a dedicated Web site to solicit ideas for funding. The board then selects

projects to be funded, and research partners convert those ideas into practical solutions.

In June 2007, the board's program for collaborative R&D had a portfolio of 600 projects with a combined investment of more than £900 million from business and government. Private firms, universities, and other research organizations can bid to cover up to 50 percent of a project's cost. These projects are evaluated on technical and economic grounds and can receive funding anywhere from £200,000 to £1 million for a two- to three-year period. The emphasis is on collaborative projects.

The board also has developed an Innovation Platforms program, which addresses major policy and societal challenges. The board identifies priority areas and looks for solutions

Table 7.1

Innovation process	Strategy
Establishing priorities	Cultivate (Technology strategy board)
Generating ideas	Network (Collaborative R&D, Innovation platforms)
Selecting ideas	Cultivate (Technology strategy board)
Implementation	Network, partner
Diffusion	Network, partner (Knowledge transfer networks/ Knowledge transfer partnership)

from the private sector. The pilot projects focused on Intelligent Transport Systems and Services and Network Security. Since then, three more priority areas have been added: Low Carbon Vehicles, Assisted Living, and Low Impact Buildings. The Intelligent Transport Systems and Services project has coordinated more than £34 million to create a holistic solution to the country's transportation challenges, particularly issues associated with traffic congestion, traffic network management, crime, infrastructure, and user travel information.

The board accomplishes diffusion through two mechanisms. The first is the Knowledge Transfer Network, which brings together individuals from academia, business, finance, and technology to generate innovations, facilitate knowledge exchange, and inform the government about issues that advance or stall innovation, such as regulations. Lack of access to information and technology is considered the greatest obstacle that businesses face in embracing innovation. Net-

works help stimulate the flow of knowledge, information, and people across players (firms, universities, research organizations, customers, suppliers) and sectors. So far, the technology board has spawned 22 knowledge transfer networks involving more than 13,000 people.

The second mechanism is the Knowledge Transfer Partnership, which enables a company to improve its performance by collaborating on projects with a knowledge partner, such as a university. The technology board bears the costs of the knowledge partner's participation.

As government agencies tackle their innovation challenges, they would do well to take an integrated and systemic approach across the continuum of five strategies and four stages of innovation. Designing a system that encourages innovation and enables the organization to execute new ideas requires a systemic view of the innovation process (figure 7.4). The strategies do not operate in silos. Moreover, multiple strategies work in unison, at various stages of the innovation cycle, to take an idea all the

Figure 7.4: An integrated innovation life cycle map

Degree of external sourcing

	Cultivate	Replicate	Partnership	Network	Open source
Idea generation	• Skunk works • Tacit knowledge of employees • Intrapreneurs • New collaboration tools (e.g., wikis)	• Review commissions • Policy entrepreneurs	• Buy innovations from best-in-class providers • Partners as "knowledge brokers" • Silo busting	• Idea scouts • Suppliers • Proprietary networks • External networks • Citizen innovators	• Any source but mainly users
Idea selection	• Innovation markets • Employee prediction markets • Skunk works	• Criteria for selection – simple, voluntary participation, tied to goals and "ideals"	• Create metrics • Gain funds • Define mutual benefits and goals	• Prediction markets • Studio process (deep needs of citizens) • Citizen participation	• Users • Dispute settlement mechanisms • Centralized control
Idea conversion	• Create safe havens • Encourage "Intrapreneurs" • Provide incentives (performance pay, gainsharing) • Accept failures • Develop capabilities of frontline employees	• Adapt to local context • Manage stakeholders	• Use innovative public private partnership models • Share risks and costs • Acquire culture • Acquire channels • Share-in-savings	• New delivery mechanisms • One-stop portals to a myriad of services • Communication and knowledge management	• Build infrastructure • Provide free access • Create flexibility in use • Provide support
Diffusion	• Manage risks • Awards and recognition	• Interlocking networks • Communities of practice • Informal groups • Awards program	• Benefit from transborder networks • Adopt innovations simultaneously • Exchange employees • Manage internal stakeholders	• Social networks • Agency networks	• Generate interest from users and participants • Provide financial sustainability

Life cycle

way through implementation and diffusion.

The innovation process has been ill defined and irregular in the public sector. By focusing on the innovation cycle, public sector managers can use a mix of strategies to suit their particular needs — say, networking for idea generation, cultivation for idea selection, partnership for idea implementation, and networks for diffusion. A specific strategy may work best for a particular organization at any stage in the innovation cycle.

To build a strategy for innovation, managers need to look at the entire innovation process and strengthen the weakest link. Getting better at the part of the innovation process where an agency already excels merely builds greater pressure at the "bottleneck" — the part where the agency doesn't excel — without creating a systemic improvement. Government organizations that want systemic improvement by adopting new innovation strategies will have to become adept at managing innovation through its cycle.

Capabilities versus strategies

Outward-looking innovation strategies require different capabilities from internally-driven processes (see figure 7.5). Information sharing, coordination, and dispute resolution are essential skills for achieving success with network and open source strategies. Compared to traditional models, these new methods pose unique management and technological challenges. For instance, implementing a networked approach required CSIRO to centralize all support services and overhaul its organizational structure to improve coordination. The organization also needed new software to maintain network ties and track results. Wikipedia's open source model requires formal and informal mechanisms to resolve disputes.

Information sharing and coordination are easier with internally oriented strategies like cultivation, but agencies need to possess the right resources, skills, and risk management abilities in order to be successful. Building these internal capabilities can be challenging, especially with shrinking budgets. Traditional strategies, particularly cultivate, work best for organizations that need innovations related to their core activities, and these activities are so specialized that employees have more competency and experience than external sources. Employees at TSA, for example, who submit innovative ideas to the "Idea Factory," leverage the tacit knowledge gained through years of working in the field. This kind of experience can be difficult to replicate from the outside world.

Perhaps the best course for organizations is to seek a balance between internal and external innovation sources. External ideas can be extremely valuable, but ignoring or under-investing in internal capabilities can be a recipe for disaster. Private sector companies like Proctor & Gamble try to maintain a ratio that is about fifty-fifty.

Flatten organization

Rigid and opaque structures that foster a culture of acquiescence rather than change typi-

120

Figure 7.5 Capability versus strategies

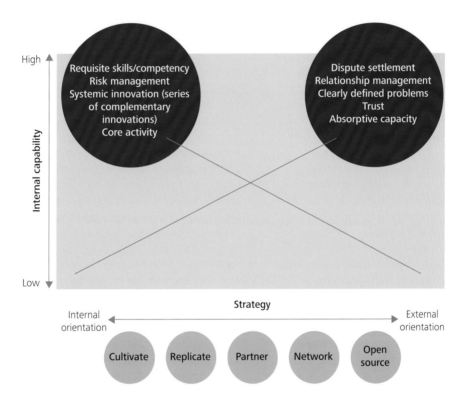

cally will not sustain innovative performance. They also make it harder to attract and retain talent. And a talent shortage is something public agencies can ill afford at a time when vast numbers of baby boomers are expected to retire, leaving big holes in government organizations. (In numerous surveys, for example, today's college students interested in making a difference say they favor working for non-

profit organizations over the public sector. The major reason why: Excessive bureaucracy.)[100]

Many of the workplace values most important to Generation Y — the generational cohort born between 1979 and 2000 that is expected to replace the retiring baby boomers — align quite well with public sector work. For example, Gen Y demonstrates a notable preference for job mobility within a single organization as opposed to the open market.[101] However, the image of the public sector as a slow-moving, bureaucratic monolith, juxtaposed against a fast-moving, anti-bureaucratic Gen Y, poses a significant challenge. Sixty percent of college students identify the nonprofit sector as better at spending money wisely, compared with government. Moreover, 76 percent cite the nonprofit sector as better at helping people; only 16 percent say the government is better.[102]

Against this backdrop, public sector agencies are experimenting with innovative practices to make themselves an employer of choice among the emerging Generation Y. For example, the Ministry of Refugee, Immigration, and Integration Affairs in Denmark started a pilot project in 2006–07 that chose 13 head clerks with strategic skills to be coached and mentored into future leaders.

Mobility across jobs, projects, and teams stimulates commitment from employees. The Chinese government provides considerable flexibility to new recruits in selecting jobs that match their career plans and needs. It invests in improving competencies within its young talent pool through training and even temporary leadership positions in public agencies.

These incremental improvements, however, do not offer a magic wand for recruiting and retaining the next generation of innovative-minded government employees. In the words of strategy guru Gary Hamel, "All too often, the risk-reward trade-off for internal entrepreneurs is long on risk and short on reward."[103] If this is true of the private sector,

it is certainly true of the public sector. "You can look at retention rates, but that's only part of the story" continues Hamel. "People often quit emotionally long before they quit physically. Novelty, meaning, and impact are the oxygen that gives life to the entrepreneurial spirit. Denied that oxygen, even the most talented folks are soon brain dead."[104]

The public sector must offer an environment that fulfills the main reason why many employees joined in the first place: making a difference in the lives of people. This will often mean tapping into the enthusiasm and optimism of young adults, helping them to realize their career aspirations.

Denmark's Ministry of Trade and Industry confronted these issues in the 1990s. Handicapped by its rigid, top-down organizational structure, the ministry struggled to meet the challenges posed by globalization and migration. Further, the organization had little chance of attracting a new generation of talented employees who had little enthusiasm for working in command-and-control organizations.

The ministry made a massive shift in 1997, replacing its strict chain of command with a project-based management structure where responsibility is broadly distributed.[105] Employees were grouped into three competence centers based on their educational background, and project groups are now created by selecting employees from these centers. No single person serves as the project leader. Instead all project group members share responsibility for the task. Managers coordinate

DEFRA's flexible staffing matches skills to tasks

The new approach of the Department for Environment, Food and Rural Affairs (DEFRA) in the United Kingdom to managing performance, illustrated in the figure below, expands the definition of "talent" to encompass all employee groups including front-line operational staff and uses skills profiles, as opposed to job descriptions, to catalogue abilities and experience. A dedicated IT-based skill repository provides information on the skills and capabilities of departmental employees. Resource managers consult this repository to match tasks to employees based on their expertise and availability. The new system has helped improve productivity by reducing downtime between projects. It has also brought in a new matrix structure that addresses three critical issues of a perfor-

mance management system: matching skills to tasks at hand, upgrading the skills of individual employees, and managing project performance. While resource managers match skills to tasks, specific managers are assigned to oversee career development of individual employees. In addition, project managers assume responsibility for individual assignments and activities. This private sector model of flexible resource planning is underpinned by a new culture and technology.

Cultural issues involve how employees view these changes. Employees need to see the new structures as efficient systems for managing skills and performance, rather than a means to park nonperforming workers in common pools. Organizations must cultivate this positive view through change support and clear communication; otherwise reforms can be undermined by workforce resistance.

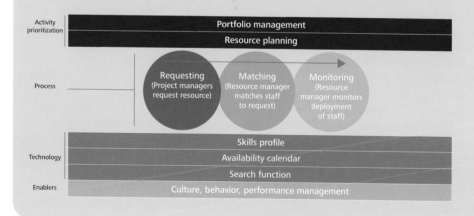

among the groups and coach employees.

The new organizational structure produced impressive results. The ministry now is a preferred career destination for economics students, and around 90 percent of current employees say they like their work environment and see opportunities for advancement. The changes also improved productivity: Staff resources devoted to meeting the day-to-day requirements of the minister dropped from 50 percent to 30 percent.[106] The ministry was renamed the Ministry of Economic and Business Affairs in November 2001, when it absorbed the tasks of three other ministries.

Create a culture of innovation

Organizations trying to build new capacities and devise new ways of conducting business need to change the prevailing culture — the beliefs, behaviors, and assumptions that have accumulated over time. As Daryl Conner, a leading expert on change management says: "Whenever a discrepancy exists between the current culture and objectives of change, the culture always wins."[107]

Culture is transmitted through both formal means (such as rules, regulations, and hierarchies) and informal means (such as norms, unofficial guidelines, and casual conversation). For example, the public accountability culture in the public sector has often meant that routines and processes take precedence over innovation and outcomes. External scrutiny can cause government employees to shrink from introduc-

ing any changes that might possibly make them the subject of a negative headline.

Add to this a deeply ingrained culture of accepting mediocre and poor performance that has prevented public sector organizations from instituting better reward systems that link productivity and pay, from sharing responsibility for performance between political figures and individual managers, and from confronting poor performance head on. A survey conducted in the United Kingdom revealed that 63 percent of government employees believe that their organization's culture tolerates low performance.[108] A culture that pays lip service to performance typically means that few informal mechanisms for discussing performance are in place.

Therefore, the first step in creating a culture of innovation is defining a shared vision. This vision should be a concrete statement of what your organization wants to achieve, such as "putting a man on the moon in 10 years." The next step is assessing your organization's current capabilities against that vision and identifying gaps that must be filled. At this point, managing cultural change becomes crucial, such as addressing employee concerns that create fear and resistance. Employees may worry about building new competencies, and they may fear potential job loss. Managers can find it stressful to raise expectations and communicate them. Be prepared to accept failures and provide support to develop new skills. The road to achieving a vision often involves some experimentation and setbacks along the way.

Pushing the culture: British Columbia's innovation action plan

The Canadian province of British Columbia (BC) launched a major innovation initiative after employee surveys revealed several roadblocks to implementing new ideas. According to the surveys, employees felt they had neither the permission nor the means to innovate. Communication was another barrier, with employees saying they lacked sufficient information to propose transformative ideas.

To overcome these challenges, the BC Public Service took a series of steps to instill a culture of innovation throughout the organization. First, the province defined its values. A new brand statement "Where Ideas Work" signaled the aspiration to encourage new ideas and to act upon them. Core values, including courage, curiosity, passion, accountability, service, and teamwork, were identified in consultation with employees.

Further, senior executives were subject to bonuses and salary holdbacks of a minimum of 10 percent based on their demonstrated support for innovation and employee engagement. Annual employee innovation awards also were created, and the BC Public Service began aggressively seeking external awards to gain recognition and, thus, attract more innovators.

Other activities include organizing "Innovation Sessions" where employee focus groups examine what they need to become more innovative. These suggestions are inventoried and turned into a comprehensive list of scalable ideas that are implemented within a year. Further, corporate values related to innovation, such as courage and curiosity, will be factored into every employee's performance assessment.

Conclusion

Talk to a management expert and she will tell you that the bureaucratic management style is an important tool in any manager's armory of capabilities. Any organization, whether private or public, has rules, procedures, and processes that need to be adhered to. But bureaucracies are also often inefficient, slow, and unresponsive, and they are not known to promote innovations. If a hierarchy is the only, or the primary, style of management used in an organization, it likely disconnects employees from their goals and blocks creativity and performance.

Promoting an innovative government requires an organization and governance model that taps all the sources of innovation available to governments to identify, adopt, adapt, and diffuse creative ideas. To tap all these sources — employees, citizens, businesses, and non-profits — governments can turn to five strategies, ranging from the cultivation strategy for change to the outward-focused open source model of innovation. To excel at innovation, governments must use the appropriate mix of strategies based on the specific challenges they face and then manage innovations from idea generation through selection, implementation, and diffusion. This entails moving beyond the "idea equals innovation" model to embrace the process of converting "best ideas into practice."

Some of the five strategies may conflict with the existing organizational structure and culture in government organizations. Proper execution of innovation will require government organizations to move from hierarchy to inclusion; from ownership to collaboration; from invention to adaptation; and from a culture of acquiescence to a culture of performance. This transition may involve rethinking organizational boundaries, acquiring new capabilities to better manage the innovation process, and creating flatter, less siloed organizations with a culture focused on performance.

When governments can do all of this successfully, the day may come when no one mistakes the term "innovative government" for an oxymoron.

126

Chapter in a box

Without altering traditional roles, processes, and organizational structures, innovation initiatives can become mired in bureaucracy and fail to deliver fundamental change. Some changes in organizational structures and culture are often necessary to make optimal use of innovation strategies.

Redefine organizational boundaries. Proctor & Gamble and CSIRO developed networked approaches designed to collect ideas from external sources and develop holistic solutions. Both cases involved forging relationships with multiple organizations and individuals in order to gain a new window into the world. P&G used proprietary and external networks to identify good ideas. CSIRO created the Flagship program, a network of organizations tied to broad thematic issues and held together through a new management structure and technology.

Take an integrated view: Multiple innovation strategies work in unison to take an idea to market. The Technology Strategy Board in the United Kingdom, for example, uses multiple strategies to translate knowledge residing in various organizations into innovations. The board consults with members of the private sector to set priorities and uses a dedicated Web site to solicit funding ideas. The board then selects projects to be funded, and research partners convert those ideas into practical solutions. To diffuse these solutions, the board created 22 knowledge transfer networks involving more than 13,000 people.

Flatten organization. The United Kingdom's Department for Environment, Food and Rural Affairs (DEFRA) initiated an integrated approach to performance management. Employees are grouped into a series of competencies based on skill sets defined by training and experience, and project groups are created by selecting employees from these groups. Managers coordinate among the groups and coach employees.

Create a culture of innovation. The British Columbia Public Service is reshaping its organizational culture to overcome barriers to innovation. The organization defined core organization values in consultation with employees and issued a brand statement "Where Ideas Work" to encourage the flow of ideas and attract innovators. Future activities to promote cultural change include organizing "Innovation Sessions" where employee focus groups study how they can become more innovative.

Appendix

"An innovation, to be effective, has to be simple and it has to be focused. It should do only one thing, otherwise it confuses. If it is not simple, it won't work. Everything new runs into trouble; if complicated, it cannot be repaired or fixed. All effective innovations are breathtakingly simple. Indeed, the greatest praise an innovation can receive is for people to say: 'This is obvious. Why didn't I think of it?'"

Peter F. Drucker

Frequently asked questions

What can we do right now to encourage innovation?

Step #1: Define what innovation means in the context of your organization. Are you looking to increase your revenues, reduce costs, improve service delivery, or all of the above? Without a benchmark to validate their ideas, employees will likely find it difficult to suggest innovative ideas, and when they do, they will not know how ideas will be evaluated. It will also be difficult to secure innovations from external sources. This is why organizations such as Tesco have clearly defined what they mean by innovation. An idea has to meet three criteria to be considered innovative: better for customers, simpler for staff, and less expensive for Tesco (page 35).

Step #2: Help employees create a business case for their ideas. Frontline employees, many having spent a greater part of their working life performing routine jobs in an insulated environment, might not have the skills and acumen required to prepare and present a business case. This was the greatest challenge facing the U.S. Forest Service when it launched the Enterprise Program to promote intrapreneurs (page 45). The In-house R&D Network at the Bureau of Motor Equipment of the New York City Department of Sanitation overcame this by enlisting bureau analysts to help develop the business case for each project (page 35).

Step #3: Decide who takes responsibility for implementing ideas. Some ideas can be left to employees to implement. For example, the In-House R&D Network allows worksite committees of mechanics to adopt proposals and implement changes within the scope of their operations (page 35).

Step #4: Diffuse successful pilots throughout the organization. Programs with proven track records tend to meet less resistance than untried ideas (page 28). Agencies can build on past successes. One example is the "innovation exchange" program between the city of London and New York City (page 20).

Step #5: Develop the skills and competencies to innovate. Top leadership should pay attention to developing the requisite competencies in frontline employees. To make partnering a "way of life," the U.S. Department of the Interior sends employees to work in locations that excel at collaboration (page 69).

How do we incentivize innovations?

#1: Reward innovators. Employee appreciation, award programs, and external recognition can all stimulate the innovation process. Frontline employees can be given financial incentives in the form of bonuses, commissions, and gainsharing. Also important is the intellectual stimulation offered by a challenging work environment and satisfaction gained in meeting the larger objective of serving the public purpose (page 122). Senior executives can be given bonuses for showing commitment and support to innovation and employees, as the province of British Columbia has done (page 125).

#2: Employ strategies to encourage innovation from partners and networks.
- Generate and share revenues through partnerships that meet common goals (page 71).
- Lend money and credibility to nonprofits that reach out to the community through government agencies to promote community-centered innovations (page 69).
- Use grant money. The Science & Technology Directorate in the Department of Homeland Security (DHS) develops formal relationships with academia, state and local governments, other public agencies, and private organizations like Google and Apple to test and prototype emerging technologies (page 80). Government organizations can also fund networks for innovation.
- Seed organizations such as In-Q-Tel to organize innovation networks (page 82).

#3: Encourage citizens to contribute innovations to public projects. This challenge is to develop and organize communities around important issues to serve a public purpose. Future Melbourne used extensive consultation and discussion with citizens to raise interest in creating a shared vision (page 103). The District of Columbia Government organized a contest to create incentives to use open source tools to help governments improve performance and responsiveness (page 105).

What can leaders do to encourage innovation?

Defining the organizational mission is often a leadership issue; it requires a fresh look at the role of the public sector agency and strong political will to change it. As the Thatcher government in the United Kingdom demonstrated in the 1980s, it generally takes a very clear mandate from the public and a strong leader to overcome vested interests (page 26). Effective leadership is also likely to be needed for less sweeping ideas, including those generated at the front-line staff or middle-manager level. This means that the role of leadership is not merely to "think" or "strategize" but also to execute.

Leaders help transmit an idea generated by an individual or a small group to the entire organization. For example, Steve Kelman, who led the initiative to reform the U.S. federal government's procurement system, estimates that around 18 percent of the employees were active advocates of the reform even before its launch (page 26).

Leaders also help frontline employees build the business case for change, provide necessary resources, and remain involved in implementation. For example, when employees suggested removing some middle management positions to cut costs, then Indianapolis Mayor Goldsmith backed them (page 58). Training employees to take on the new role of intrapreneurs was an essential element of the Enterprise Program at the U.S. Forest Service (page 45).

How should we manage the risks associated with innovation?

The fear of failure and wariness of funding untested approaches pose significant challenges for innovation. Political realities drive this risk aversion — failures make headlines while successes are spread thinly, over millions of constituents. The fact that many innovations don't bear fruit within the political election cycle doesn't make things any easier.

Innovation is about experimentation. Experiments often fail. A can't-afford-to-fail environment is not very conducive to making ambitious decisions or investments. Governments need to provide incentives for risk taking and create mechanisms for calculating risk, so that the fear of failure does not trump the desire to create new initiatives.

Today, many governments suffer from big ticket failures with projects that run too long and cost too much money. In contrast, in successful organizations the motto is to "fail small, fail fast." The idea is to fail quickly if you have to, learn from the experience, and move on to the next big idea. New York City Mayor Michael Bloomberg mobilized private funds to launch innovative pilot programs before spending public money on a citywide rollout (page 68).

Others try to learn about innovations and best practices developed elsewhere and amass a rich storehouse of ideas they can adapt to their own needs. They select ideas that the organization can execute now or else build the required competencies within the organization (page 54).

Quick wins and early successes create a positive environment for new ideas. This is why Ken Miller suggests creating a buzz around successful innovations as an effective way of gaining support from the political leadership and other employees (page 27). Building on past successes helps to avoid early adopter mistakes (page 104).

How do we find the time to innovate when we're already overloaded trying to fulfill our basic responsibilities?

Organizations need to create time for employees to reflect on what they are doing and why, and to take up projects that add more value. Otherwise, innovation will remain a top-down management exercise. Pioneering companies such as Google and 3M allow their employees to spend close to 20 percent of their time developing their own business ideas (page 44).

Another option is to create safe havens — separate units kept close to mainstream activities but away from line organizations — to permit low-risk experimentation. Skunk works, a type of safe haven, are composed of small groups of highly talented and motivated people who are freed from bureaucracy, paper work, and most routine administrative responsibilities (page 43). The Technology Strategy Board in the United Kingdom is a good example of a skunk work to promote innovation (page 117–118). The U.S. Department of Homeland Security's Science & Technology Directorate has created a special center to work with outside partners on innovation.

How can we integrate innovation strategies and practices into day-to-day management and service delivery?

#1. Create an innovation culture. The beliefs, behaviors, and assumptions that have accumulated over time together form the culture of an organization. These are transmitted as much through formal means (rules and regulations) as through informal means (norms, guidelines, and casual conversation). If you create new rules but make no effort to change the informal structures, employees will likely not change their behavior (page 124). The British Columbia Public Service has tried to instill a culture of innovation throughout the organization using everything from organizing "Innovation Sessions" where employee focus groups examine what they need to become more innovative, to defining the new brand statement for the organization as being "Where Ideas Work" (page125).

#2: Smash the silos. Many public sector organizations are looking at creating flexible performance management systems through tools such as "surplus pools," or placing employees in common pools (instead of remaining stuck in divisional silos) between projects from where they can be allocated to other projects.

#3: Follow through on the execution of the innovation. Leaders also need to demonstrate their support to employee initiatives. This means taking a systems view of the innovation process; merely focusing on idea generation without an efficient process to select and implement ideas will impede the innovation process. TSA's idea factory provides a good example of expecting innovation (page 40).

#4: Don't punish well-meaning failures. Managers need to be deeply aware of the risk-averse nature of the public sector environment. Overhauling this culture will require continuous leadership support and an acceptance of failure. The idea of "fail small, fail fast" will need to be drilled down from the top to the bottom (page 42). Flexibility in shifting project priorities and methodology will allow employees to highlight problems early on, rather than hide them until they turn into mammoth failures.

Good sources on innovation

Government innovation:

Innovations in Government: Research, Recognition, and Replication (ed), Sanford Borins (Brookings Press, 2008).

William D. Eggers, *Government 2.0: Using Technology to Improve Education, Cut Red Tape, Reduce Gridlock, and Enhance Democracy* (Rowman and Littlefield, 2005).

Mark A. Abramson and Ian D. Littman (eds), *Innovation*, (Rowman and Littlefield, 2002).

David Osborne and Peter Plastrik, *The Reinventor's Fieldbook: Tools for Transforming Your Government* (Jossey-Bass, 2000).

John Donahue, *Making Washington Work: Tales of Innovation in the Federal Government* (Brookings Press, 1999).

Stephen Goldsmith, *The Twenty-First Century City* (Regnery Gateway, 1997).

David Osborne and Peter Plastrik, *Banishing Bureaucracy: The Five Strategies for Reinventing Government* (Basic Books, 1997).

John Kao, *Innovation Nation: How America Is Losing Its Innovation Edge, Why It Matters, and What We Can Do to Get It Back* (Free Press, 2007).

Business Innovation:

Tom Kelley, *The Ten Faces of Innovation* (Broadway Books, 2005); and *The Art of Innovation: Lessons in Creativity from IDEO, America's Leading Design Firm* (Broadway Books, 2001).

Clayton Christensen, *Innovators Dilemma: When New Technologies Cause Great Firms to Fail* (Harvard Business School Press, 2009); and (with Michael Raynor) *Innovators Solution: Creating and Sustaining Successful Growth* (Harvard Business School Press, 2003).

Bernd H. Schmitt, *Big Think Strategy: How to Leverage Bold Ideas and Leave Small Thinking Behind* (Harvard Business School Press, 2007).

Peter F. Drucker, *Innovation and Entrepreneurship: Practice and Principles* (HarperCollins, 1985).

Gary Hamel, *Leading the Revolution* (Harvard Business School Press, 2002).

John Hagel III and John Seely Brown, *The Only Sustainable Edge: Why Business Strategy Depends on Productive Friction and Dynamic Specialization* (Harvard Business School Press, 2005).

Idea Generation

Chip Heath and Dan Heath, *Made to Stick: Why Some Ideas Survive and Others Die* (Random House, 2007).

Jack Foster, *How to Get Ideas* (Berrett-Koehler Publishers, 2007).

William Duggan, *Strategic Intuition: The Creative Spark in Human Achievement* (New York: Columbia University Press, 2007).

Networks and innovation:

Stephen Goldsmith and William D. Eggers, *Governing by Network* (Brookings Press, 2004).

Don Tapscott and Anthony D. Williams, *Wikinomics: How Mass Collaboration Changes Everything* (Portfolio, 2006).

Ilkka Tuomi, *Networks of Innovation: Change and Meaning in the Age of the Internet*, (Oxford University Press, 2006).

Satish Nambisan, *The Global Brain: Your Roadmap for Innovating Faster & Smarter in a Networked World* (Wharton School Publishing, 2007).

Michael Tushman and Charles A. O'Reilly, *Winning through Innovation: A Practical Guide to Leading Organizational Change and Renewal* (Harvard Business School Press, 1997).

Open source and open innovation:

Eric Von Hippel, *Democratizing Innovation* (The MIT Press, 2005).

Stephen Weber, *The Success of Open Source* (Harvard University Press, 2005).

Henry Chesbrough, *Open Innovation: The New Imperative for Creating and Profiting from Technology* (Harvard Business School Press, 2003); *Open Business Models: How to Thrive in the New Innovation Landscape* (Harvard Business School Press, 2006); and *Open Innovation: Researching a New Paradigm* (Oxford University Press, 2006).

Georg von Krogh, Kazuo Ichijo, and Ikujiro Nonaka, *Enabling Knowledge Creation: How to Unlock the Mystery of Tacit Knowledge and Release the Power of Innovation* (Oxford University Press, 2000).

Publications:

Governing (www.governing.com)
Government Executive (www.govexec.com)
Canadian Government Executive (http://www.networkedgovernment.ca/)
Harvard Business Review (http://harvardbusinessonline.hbsp.harvard.edu/)
Sloan Management Review (http://sloanreview.mit.edu/)

Organizations:

Ash Institute for Democratic Governance (http://ashinstitute.harvard.edu/)
Institute for Large Scale Innovation (www.largescaleinnovation.org)

Web sites:

Government Innovators Network (http://www.innovations.harvard.edu)
Harvard Business School Press (http://www.hbsp.harvard.edu/)
Edge Perspectives with John Hagel (http://edgeperspectives.typepad.com/edge_perspectives/).

Endnotes

[1] Tom Kelly, *The Ten Faces of Innovation* (New York: Doubleday, 2005), p. 5.

[2] Jessica McDonald, "Getting Serious about Public Service Innovation," *Canadian Government Executive Magazine*, March 2008, accessed January 19, 2009 < http://www.netgov.ca/cp.asp?pid=104>.

[3] Sharon Dawes, "Breaching the Wall: A Lesson in Leadership," *Government Technology*, February 2007.

[4] Morten T. Hansen and Julian Birkinshaw, "The Innovation Value Chain," *Harvard Business Review*, June 2007, p. 101.

[5] "New York City, London Announce 'Innovation Exchange' Program," *Government Technology*, May 9, 2008, accessed May 19, 2008 <http://www.govtech.com/gt/articles/320843?id=&story_pg=1>.

[6] Bernd H. Schmitt, *Big Think Strategy: How To Leverage Bold Ideas and Leave Small Thinking Behind* (Cambridge, MA: Harvard Business School Press, 2007), p. 39.

[7] Robert Chapman Wood and Gary Hamel, "The World Bank's Innovation Market," *Harvard Business Review*, November 2002, p. 104–113.

[8] Global Alliance for Vaccines and Immunization, "Global Results," accessed June 4, 2008 <http://www.gavialliance.org/performance/global_results/index.php>.

[9] Steve Towns, "Vivek Kundra, CTO of Washington, D.C., Focuses on Project Management," Government Technology, July 9, 2008 <http://www.govtech.com/pcio/articles/375806>.

[10] U.S. Congress Office of Technology of Assessment, "Teachers and Technology: Making the Connections," OTA-HER-616, Washington, DC: U.S. Government Printing Office, April 1995, p. 74.

[11] Paul Macmillan, "Moving Forward: Promoting Innovative Government for Long-Term Success," Deloitte & Touche LLP, 2008, p. 6.

[12] Steven J. Kelman, "Changing Big Government Organizations: Easier than Meets the Eye?," Faculty Research Working Paper Series RWP04-026, John F. Kennedy School of Government, Harvard University, May 2004.

[13] Ken Miller, "Guerilla Warfare: How to Create Change When You Are Not in Charge," Governing.com, July 12, 2007 <http://www.governing.com/articles/7kmiller.htm>.

[14] Jena McGregor et al., "The World's Most Innovative Companies," *BusinessWeek*, April 24, 2006, Issue 3981, pp. 63–74.

15 National Audit Office, "Achieving Innovations in Central Government Organizations," July 25, 2007, p. 24.

16 TESCO, "Every Little Helps," Corporate Social Responsibility Review 2002-03, p. 17 <http://www.tescocorporate.com/images/TescoCSRreview03_1.pdf>.

17 Ibid., 26.

18 Arnold M. Howitt, "Engaging Frontline Employees in Organizational Renewal," Occasional Paper 2-97, The Innovations in American Government Program, John F. Kennedy School of Government, Harvard University, Fall 1997, p. 2.

19 Kathleen Teltsch, "Sanitation Department is Honored for Innovation," *New York Times*, September 23, 1992 <http://query.nytimes.com/gst/fullpage.html?res=9E0CE3DC113FF930A1575AC0A964958260&sec=&spon=&pagewanted=1>.

20 Rachael King, "Hollywood Games People Play," *BusinessWeek*, August 7, 2006 <http://www.businessweek.com/technology/content/aug2006/tc20060804_618481.htm>.

21 Emile Servan-Schreiber, Justin Wolfers, David M. Pennock, and Brian Galebach, "Prediction Markets: Does Money Matter," in Andreas Herman et al., *EM-Electronic Markets*, 14(3), September 2004 <http://www.newsfutures.com/pdf/Does_money_matter.pdf>.

22 James M. Pethokoukis, "All Seeing All Knowing," *U.S. News and World Report*, August 22, 2004 <http://www.usnews.com/usnews/biztech/articles/040830/30forecast_2.htm>.

23 Leslie Walker, "Uncle Sam Wants Napster," *Washington Post*, November 8, 2001, p. E01, <http://www.washingtonpost.com/ac2/wp-dyn?pagename=article&node=washtech/techthursday/columns/dotcom&contentId=A59099-2001Nov7>.

24 James Cartwright, Joint Chiefs of Staff Vice Chairman, *Government Computer News*, October 12, 2007 <http://www.gcn.com/print/26_30/45517-1.html>.

25 A trim tab is of great value for massive ocean-going vessels that build up so much momentum that it is difficult to move the rudder without a very real risk of breaking it. Turning the trim tab creates a low pressure and eases the big rudder around. Trim tabs are also used to control the upward and downward lift on airplanes and boats, bringing the nose down for increased speed and raising the nose to reduce speed. Small boats use trim tabs to compensate for weight distribution and speed (the reason why at times passengers are asked to move up or down the boat by the boater).

142

[26] Peter M. Senge, *The Fifth Discipline: The Art and Practice of the Learning Organization* (London: Random House, 2006), p. 58.

[27] William D. Eggers and John O'Leary, *Revolution at the Roots: Making Our Government Smaller, Better, and Closer to Home* (New York: Free Press, 1995).

[28] New Zealand has been ahead of other governments in using performance-for-pay systems to improve productivity in government. There are also a number of awards given for innovation in government — the National Performance Review Hammer Awards and the Ford Foundation Innovation in American Governments award are some examples from the United States.

[29] Patrick J. Keogh, "Spiff Up Employee Incentives," *Government Executive*, February 1, 1998 <http://www.govexec.com/features/0298mgmt.htm>.

[30] Spiff, as discussed here, refers to special performance incentives or cash awards to employees for creating savings.

[31] Stefan Thomke, "Enlightened Experimentation: The New Imperative for Innovation," *Harvard Business Review*, February, 2001, p. 71.

[32] Gautham Nagesh, "Fostering Innovation," *Government Executive*, April 9, 2008 <http://www.govexec.com/dailyfed/0408/040908mm.htm>.

[33] This Center is a 1995 winner of the Innovations in American Government Award.

[34] Center for Technology in Government, *Advancing Digital Government Research: 06 Annual Report*, University at Albany, State University of New York, 2007, p. 22. CTG has also developed a public value framework for governments to assess whether the public returns from an IT investment are big enough to justify the investment. The framework explicitly recognizes the failure of traditional return-on-investment analysis in a public sector context. It incorporates the political (ability to influence government action or policy) and ideological (moral or ethical positions and commitments) impact of new IT investment to develop a more comprehensive measure of public value.

[35] Gifford Pinchot, *Intrapreneuring: Why You Don't Have to Leave the Organization to Become an Entrepreneur*, (New York: Harper and Row, 1985).

[36] Toni L. Stafford, "The U.S. Forest Service Enterprise Program: Reinvigorating Government," *Forest History Today*, Spring/Fall 2007, p. 42.

[37] Jeffrey L. Bradach, "Going to Scale: The Challenge of Replicating Social Programs," *Stanford Social Innovation Review*, Spring 2003, p. 19 <http://www.ssireview.org/images/articles/2003SP_feature_bradach.pdf>.

38 Louis Winnick, "Is Reinventing Government Enough?" *City Journal*, Summer 1993 <http://www.city-journal.org/article01.php?aid=1470>.

39 Ellen Perlman, "Stephen Goldsmith: Busting the Government Monopoly," *Governing*, December 1995 <http://www.governing.com/archive/1995/dec/poy.txt>.

40 For example, when the Alaska pipeline was near completion in 1976, Alaska created a permanent fund to collect 25 percent of mineral proceeds. For governments that have seen no similar surge in revenue from natural resources, this innovation is irrelevant.

41 "Home Improvements: A Manual for Conducting Performance Reviews," Texas Performance Review <http://www.window.state.tx.us/tpr/home/t31.html>.

42 Oscar Monteiro, "Institutional and Organizational Restructuring of the Civil Service in Developing Countries," Paper 1, The Fourth Global Forum on Reinventing Government: Capacity Development Workshops, Marakkech, Morocco, December 10–11, 2002 <http://unpan1.un.org/intradoc/groups/public/documents/UN/UNPAN006350.pdf>.

43 Zhang Jun, "Triggering the Economic Reform in Post-Reform China: What Have We Known?," Sponsored by Brenthurst Foundation, Paper for Conference on Globalisation and Economic Success: Policy Option for Africa, Cairo, November 13–14, 2006, p. 6.

44 Frances Stokes Berry, "Innovation in Public Management: The Adoption of Strategic Planning," *Public Administration Review*, 54: 322, July/August 1994.

45 Gerald F. Davis and Henrich R. Greve, "Corporate Elite Network and Governance Changes in the 1980s," *American Journal of Sociology*, 103: 1, July 1997.

46 Malcolm Gladwell, *Blink: The Power of Thinking Without Thinking* (New York: Little, Brown and Company, 2005).

47 Lisa Arthur, "Miami Homeless Program to Go National," *Miami Herald*, September 21, 2007.

48 Governor's Communications Office, "Pacific Coast leaders build regional collaboration," Press Release, The State of Washington, June 30, 2008, accessed November 22, 2008 <http://www.governor.wa.gov/news/news-view.asp?pressRelease=938&newsType=1>.

49 William D. Eggers and Tom Startup, *Closing the Infrastructure Gap: The Role of Public-Private Partnerships*, Deloitte Research, 2006.

144

50 Peter Judge, "Linux Opens London's Oyster," ZDNet, May 22, 2008, accessed August 1, 2008 <http://resources.zdnet.co.uk/articles/casestudy/0,1000001994,39419829-2,00.htm>.

51 Geoffrey Segal, "Innovative Tools to Relieve Congestion and Improve Mobility," Testimony to the Arizona State Senate Committee on Transportation, February 13, 2007, accessed July 10, 2008 <https://www.reason.org/commentaries/segal_20070213.shtml>.

52 The "super peak rush hours" are priced more heavily to reduce congestion and divert traffic to other hours with available capacity. The rush hours are held constant for six months and customers are given advanced notice of these hours. Electronic variable message signs display the toll rates and allow customers to decide over a one-mile stretch whether they want to transition to the freeway. This gives customers the choice to evaluate whether they prefer to pay the toll (and cut down on 20 minutes of driving time) or use the freeway. High occupancy vehicles, with three or more occupants, are switched to special lanes where they do not have to pay the toll.

53 Robert Kolker, "How Is a Hedge Fund Like a School?" *New York Magazine*, February 13, 2006, accessed August 04, 2008 <http://nymag.com/news/businessfinance/15958/>.

54 Grameen Foundation, Impacting Poverty Around the World, 2005 Annual Report, Washington DC, p. 19 <http://www.grameenfoundation.org/docs/resource_center/GrameenFoundation-AnnualReport2005.pdf>.

55 U.S. Department of the Interior. "Advancing Cooperative Conservation: A Presentation to the Management Initiative Team, U.S. Department of the Interior," February 10, 2005.

56 With less than 35 percent of residents having a car, the transit stop was essential to meet the travel needs of the community and protect the economic prospects of the neighborhood struggling with high unemployment. Jennifer G. Propoky, "In Chicago, Concrete Creates New Opportunities," *Environmental Design + Construction*, September 16, 2005, accessed July 28, 2008 <http://www.edcmag.com/CDA/Articles/Concrete_Supplement/72ff85e92e697010VgnVCM100000f932a8c0>.

57 The "smart green" building has become a national model, incorporating a green roof that reduces heat absorption in summer and heat loss in winter, photovoltaic cells, automatic light dimmers, and a walking bridge connection to the Lake Street El platform.

146

[58] U.S. Environmental Protection Agency, "National Award for Smart Growth Achievement," November 2006 <http://www.epa.gov/dced/pdf/sg_awards_2006.pdf>.

[59] By not including units that KTDC already had up and running, the partners considerably reduced opposition to the joint venture from unions and other stakeholders.

[60] Ashish Kumar Singh, Interview with the authors, November 25, 2007.

[61] For example, the success of the venture with the Taj group resulted in a subsequent joint venture with another big hotel chain, the Oberoi group.

[62] "Akron, Ohio, and Summit County Collaborate on Cellular 911 Service," *Government Technology*, August 22, 2007 <http://www.govtech.com/gt/132372>.

[63] Partnerships UK, "A Guidance Note Prepared for Public Sector Bodies Forming Joint Venture Companies with the Private Sector," December 2001, p. 8.

[64] Alasdair Roberts, Transborder Service Systems: Pathways for Innovation or Threats to Accountability, Market-Based Government Series, IBM Center for the Business of Government, March 2004.

[65] "Google Developer Day London: BBC Backstage," accessed October 1, 2008 <http://www.youtube.com/watch?v=hhXD8SPqMdM>.

[66] Anthony Goerzen, "Managing Alliance Networks: Emerging Practices of Multinational Corporations," *Academy of Management Executive*, 19: 2, 2005, pp. 94–107.

[67] Larry Huston and Nabil Sakkab, "Connect and Develop: Inside Procter and Gamble's New Model for Innovation," *Harvard Business Review*, March, 2006, pp. 58–66.

[68] Eric Abrahamson and David H. Freedman, *A Perfect Mess* (New York: Little Brown and Company, 2006), p. 32.

[69] Karim R. Lakhani, Lars Bo Jeppesen, Peter A. Lohse, and Jill A. Panetta, "The Value of Openness in Scientific Problem Solving," Harvard Business School Working Papers, October 2006 <http://www.hbs.edu/research/pdf/07-050.pdf>.

[70] In-Q-Tel, "Keyhole: The Ultimate Interface to the Planet," accessed March 12, 2008 <http://www.in-q-tel.org/technology-portfolio/keyhole.html>.

[71] Robert K. Ackerman, "Intelligence Agency Seeds Technology Entrepreneurs," *SIGNAL,* April 2001, accessed January 31, 2008 <http://www.afcea.org/signal/

articles/templates/SIGNAL_Article_Template.asp?articleid=109&zoneid=31>.

72 Interview with Larry Huston, "Finding that 'Sweet Spot': A New Way to Drive Innovation," *Knowledge@Wharton*, June 27, 2007 <http://knowledge.wharton.upenn.edu/article.cfm?articleid=1765>.

73 Commonwealth Scientific and Industrial Research Organization, Annual Report 2006–07, Commonwealth of Australia, 2007, p. 7 <http://www.csiro.au/files/files/pgx5.pdf>.

74 Brad Collis, "Viewpoint: The Big Challenge," *SOLVE*, 9, November 2006, accessed September 29, 2008 <http://www.solve.csiro.au/1106/article1.htm>.

75 Interview with Larry Huston, June 27, 2007.

76 Tim Dickinson, "The Machinery of Hope," *Rolling Stone*, March 20, 2008 <http://www.rollingstone.com/news/coverstory/obamamachineryofhope>.

77 Gillian Flaccus, "1,500 homes lost; $1B loss in San Diego area," *Seattle Times*, October 24, 2007, accessed November 10, 2008 <http://seattletimes.nwsource.com/html/nationworld/2003971082_wildfires24.html>.

78 "Bush Pledges to Aid Fire-Swept California," Political Bulletin, *U.S. News & World Report*, October 24, 2007, accessed November 19, 2008 <http://www.usnews.com/usnews/politics/bulletin/bulletin_071024.htm>.

79 David Flokenflick, "KPBS Radio Covers Wildfires Using Many Sources," National Public Radio, October 26, 2007, accessed November 20, 2008 <http://www.npr.org/templates/story/story.php?storyId=15655316>.

80 Eric Von Hippel, *Democratizing Innovation* (Cambridge, MA: MIT Press, 2005).

81 Eric Von Hippel and Mary Sonnack, "Breakthroughs to Order at 3M via Lead User Innovations," MIT Sloan School of Management Working Paper 4057, January 1999 <http://dspace.mit.edu/bitstream/1721.1/2743/1/SWP-4057-42747841.pdf>.

82 My Society, FixMyStreet, accessed November 12, 2008 <http://www.mysociety.org/projects/fixmystreet/>.

83 PRO INNO Europe, "DK 35 Programme for User-driven Innovation," accessed March 17, 2008 <http://www.proinno-europe.eu/index.cfm?fuseaction=wiw.measures&page=detail&ID=9135>.

84 James Surowiecki, *The Wisdom of Crowds: Why the Many Are Smarter Than the Few and How Collective Wisdom Shapes Business, Economies, Societies and Nations* (New York: Doubleday, 2004).

85 Albert Saiz and Uri Simonsohn, "Downloading Wisdom from Online Crowds,"

SSRN <http://papers.ssrn.com/sol3/papers.cfm?abstract_id=990021>.

86 Jeffrey H. Dyer, *Collaborative Advantage: Winning Through Extended Enterprise Supplier Networks* (New York: Oxford University Press, 2000), pp. 59–83.

87 Warren E. Leary, "To the Moon, Alice! (Use Your Internet Connection, Dear)," *New York Times*, November 22, 2005, accessed November 14, 2008 <http://www.nytimes.com/2005/11/22/science/space/22moon.html?_r=2&scp=3&sq=nasa%20world%20wind&st=cse&oref=slogin&oref=slogin>.

88 Organizing an enthusiastic band of people is just one challenge that arises when organizing open source collaboration. Another is the apparent conflict between the collaboration principle and the need to protect intellectual property or maintain secrecy. Scientists, firms, and public agencies may be concerned about revealing too much information to others. Yet, a large number of organizations in the private sector are moving away from an environment of secrecy and restricted access to knowledge in a bid to create world-class systems that tackle complicated issues.

    Financial sustainability is also a pressing issue for open source communities. At the end of the day, firms and nonprofits have to pay salaries to their employees. Government agencies can take on a bigger role in using open source collaborations to meet specific needs by actively organizing these collaborative communities to innovate for them. This means the role of government agencies is not merely to buy the products developed by the open source communities but to become an organizer of challenging tasks that may be expensive, require a large number of specialists, involve ongoing support, or necessitate coordination with citizens.

89 E-Learning Ontario, "Ontario's E-Learning Strategy," December 2006 <http://www.elearningontario.ca/eng/pdf/strat_elo_en.pdf>.

90 Eric Steven Raymond, "The Cathedral and the Bazaar," <http://www.catb.org/~esr/writings/cathedral-bazaar/cathedral-bazaar/>.

91 Vivek Kundra, Remarks to the Annual Meeting of the National Academy of Public Administration, November 17, 2008.

92 Ibid.

93 Andrew Hendry, "Who's behind Wikipedia?" *ComputerWorld*, February 06, 2008, accessed May 18, 2008 <http://www.computerworld.com.au/index.php/id;1866322157;pp;1;fp;4;fpid;1968336438>.

94 Mario Biagioli, "Bringing Peer Review to Patents," *Firstmonday journal*, July

4, 2007 <http://firstmonday.org/htbin/cgiwrap/bin/ojs/index.php/fm/article/view/1868/1751>.

95 Peer to Patent Web site, accessed January 2, 2009, <http://www.peerto-patent.org/>.

96 European Commission, *Science Shops—Knowledge for the Community* (Luxembourg: Office for Official Publications of the European Communities, 2003), p. 10 <http://ec.europa.eu/research/science-society/pdf/science_shop_en.pdf>.

97 Daniel Lyons, "The Open Source Heretic," *Forbes*, May 26, 2005 <http://www.forbes.com/2005/05/26/cz_dl_0526linux.html>.

98 The Peer to Patent Project, "Beth Noveck Makes Presentation to Science in the 21st Century Conference," September 11, 2008, accessed November 20, 2008 <http://cairns.typepad.com/peertopatent/2008/09/beth-noveck-mak.html>.

99 Brad Collis, "Viewpoint: The Big Challenge," *SOLVE*, 9, November 2006, accessed September 29, 2008 < http://www.solve.csiro.au/1106/article1.htm>.

100 Peter D. Hart Research Associates, Inc., "Survey of College Students," Panetta Institute for Public Policy, Washington, June 13, 2006, p. 12.

101 The Future Workforce: Young People's Views on Career, Employers and Work, Institute for the Future, Palo Alto, California and Deloitte & Touche USA Youth Survey, January 2004.

102 Paul C. Light, Testimony before the United States Senate Governmental Affairs Committee, June 4, 2003, p. 6.

103 Gary Hamel, "Bringing Silicon Valley Inside," *Harvard Business Review*, September–October, 1999, p. 77.

104 Ibid., 82.

105 Birgit Kjoelby, "The Experience of Transforming the Ministry of Trade and Industry in Denmark into a Development Oriented Organization," *The Innovation Journal: The Public Sector Innovation Journal*, 9: 2, 2004, accessed May 19, 2008 <http://www.innovation.cc/discussion-papers/kjolby-9-2.pdf>.

106 Ibid., 9.

107 Daryl Conner, *Managing at the Speed of Change*, (New York: Random House, 1993), p.176.

108 Chiumento Consulting Group Ltd., Tough Love, Research Report, 2006, accessed May 16, 2008 <http://www.arboraglobal.com/documents/Toughlove_2006_001.pdf>.

Recent Deloitte Research public sector thought leadership

- **Mastering Finance in Government**: Transforming the Government Enterprise Through Better Financial Management
- **One Size Fits Few**: Using Customer Insight to Transform Government
- **Bolstering Human Capital**: How the Public Sector Can Beat the Coming Talent Crisis
- **Serving the Aging Citizen**
- **Closing America's Infrastructure Gap**: The Role of Public-Private Partnerships
- **Closing the Infrastructure Gap**: The Role of Public-Private Partnerships
- **States of Transition**: Tackling Government's Toughest Policy and Management Challenges
- **Building Flexibility**: New Models for Public Infrastructure Projects
- **Pushing the Boundaries**: Making a Success of Local Government Reorganization
- **Governing Forward**: New Directions for Public Leadership
- **Paying for Tomorrow**: Practical Strategies for Tackling the Public Pension Crisis
- **Medicaid Makeover**: Six Tough (and Unavoidable) Choices on the Road to Reform
- **Driving More Money into the Classroom**: The Promise of Shared Services
- **Are We There Yet**: A Roadmap for Integrating Health and Human Services
- **Government 2.0**: Using Technology to Improve Education, Cut Red Tape, Reduce Gridlock, and Enhance Democracy (Rowman and Littlefield, 2005)
- **Governing by Network**: The New Shape of the Public Sector (Brookings, 2004)
- Prospering in the Secure Economy
- **Combating Gridlock**: How Pricing Road Use Can Ease Congestion
- **Citizen Advantage**: Enhancing Economic Competitiveness through E-Government
- **Cutting Fat, Adding Muscle**: The Power of Information in Addressing Budget Shortfalls
- **Show Me the Money**: Cost-Cutting Solutions for Cash-Strapped States

151

About the authors

William D. Eggers is the Executive Director of Deloitte's Public Leadership Institute and the Global Director for Deloitte Research-Public Sector where he leads the public sector industry research program. A recognized expert on government reform, he is the author of numerous books including: *Governing by Network: The New Shape of the Public Sector* (Brookings, 2004), *Government 2.0: Using Technology to Improve Education, Cut Red Tape, Reduce Gridlock, and Enhance Democracy* (Rowman and Littlefield, 2005) and *States of Transition* (Deloitte Research 2006). He is the winner of the 2005 Louis Brownlow award for best book on public management, the 2002 APEX award for excellence in business journalism, the 1996 Roe Award for leadership and innovation in public policy research, and the 1995 Sir Antony Fisher award for best book promoting an understanding of the free economy. A former manager of the Texas Performance Review, he has advised dozens of governments around the world. His commentary has appeared in dozens of major media outlets including the *New York Times* and *Wall Street Journal*. His upcoming book, *If We Can Put a Man on the Moon*, will be published by Harvard Business School Press in the fall of 2009.

153

Shalabh Kumar Singh is an economist and has written extensively on public policy issues. Currently, his research is focused on issues that cut across public and private sector boundaries, especially applying economics to public policy and management, and bringing commercial best practices to government. He has also coauthored the book *Social Accounting Matrix for India: Concepts, Construction and Applications* (Sage Publications, 2006). He is a manager in Deloitte Research.

Public sector contacts

The following individuals represent the public sector contacts for the Deloitte Touche Tohmatsu member firms in their respective countries.

Global
Greg Pellegrino
Global Managing Director
United States
+1 617 437 2776
gpellegrino@deloitte.com

Bill Eggers
Deloitte Research Director
United States
+1 202 378 5292
weggers@deloitte.com

Peter Brown
Chief of Staff
United States
+1 202 220 2722
pdbrown@deloitte.com

Karen Lang
Marketing Director
United States
+1 517 437 2126
kalang@deloitte.com

Gemma Martin
Public Relations Director
United States
+1 212 492 4305
gemartin@deloitte.com

United States
Bob Campbell
State Sector
+1 512 226 4210
bcampbell@deloitte.com

United States
Gene Procknow
Federal Sector
+1 202 378 5190
gprocknow@deloitte.com

United States
Robin Lineberger
Federal Sector
+1 703 747 3104
rlineberger@deloitte.com

United Kingdom
Mike Turley
+44 207 303 3162
mturley@deloitte.co.uk

Australia
Rory O'Connor
+61 2 9322 7627
roroconnor@deloitt.com

Netherlands
Hans van Vliet
+31621272828
hvanvliet@deloitte.com

Canada
Paul Macmillan
+1 416 874 4203
pmacmillan@deloitte.com

Argentina
Armando Guibert
+54 11 43204022
aguibert@deloitte.com

Brazil
Edgar Jabbour
+55 11 5186 6652
ejabbour@deloitte.com

CIS
Maxim Lubomudrov
+74957870600 x3093
mlubomudrov@deloitte.ru

Austria
Gerhard Feuchtmueller
+43 1 537 00 0
gfeuchtmueller@deloitte.com

Bulgaria
Desislava Dinkova
+359 (2) 8023 182
ddinkova@deloitece.com

Cyprus
Panicos Papamichael
+357 22 360 805
ppapamichael@deloitte.com

Belgium
Hans Debruyne
+ 32 2 800 29 31
hdebruyne@deloitte.com

Central Europe
Martin Buransky
+420 246 042 349
mburansky@deloitece.com

Denmark
Hans Henrik Pontoppidan
+45 36103481
hpontoppidan@deloitte.dk

European Commission
Richard Doherty
+ 3228002916
rdoherty@deloitte.be

Finland
Lauri Byckling
+358 20 7555447
lauri.byckling@deloitte.fi

France
Gilles Pedini
+33 1 40 88 22 21
gpedini@deloitte.fr

Germany
Thomas Northoff
+49 (89) 29036 8566
tnorthoff@deloitte.de

Greece
Vasilis Pallios
+30 210 678 1100
vpallios@deloitte.gr

Hungary
Csaba Markus
+36 (1) 428 6793
csmarkus@deloittece.com

India
Kamlesh K. Mittal
+91 11 6662 2000
kamleshmittal@deloitte.com

Ireland
Gerry Fitzpatrick
+353 1 4172645
gfitzpatrick@deloitte.ie

Israel
Chaim Ben-David
+972 2 5018860
cbendavid@deloitte.co.il

Italy
Roberto Lolato
+39 0636749216
rlolato@deloitte.it

Japan
Yuji Morita
03-6213-1532
yuji.morita@tohmatsu.co.jp

Korea
Min Keun Chung
82-2-6676-3101
mchung@deloitte.com

Malaysia
Azman M. Zain
+60 3 7723 6525
azmanmzain@deloitte.com

Mexico
Enrique Clemente
+52 55 9123535
eclemente@dttmx.com

Mid Africa
Joe Eshun
+255 (22) 2116006
jeshun@deloitte.com

Middle East
Anis Jabsheh
+9626 4634605
ajabsheh@deloitte.com

New Zealand
Aloysius Teh
+64 4 495 3934
ateh@deloitte.com

Norway
Arve Hogseth
+47 95268730
ahogseth@deloitte.no

Poland
Dionizy Smolen
+48 (22) 5110292
dsmolen@deloittece.com

Portugal
Raul Mascarenhas
(+351) 210423832
ramascarenhas@deloitte.com

Singapore
Patricia Lee
+65 6216 3283
patricialee@deloitte.com

South Africa
Corne Oberholzer
+27 (0) 12 482 0244
coberholzer@deloitte.co.za

Thailand
Marasri Kanjanataweewat
+66 (0) 2676 5700
mkanjanataweewat@
deloitte.com

Spain
Gustavo Garcia Capo
+34 915145000 x2036
ggarciacapo@deloitte.es

Sweden
Johan Rasmusson
+46406696162
jrasmusson@deloitte.se

Turkey
Gokhan Alpman
+90 212 366 60 86
galpman@deloitte.com

155